Ready...
Aim...
Fire!

Small Arms Ammunition in the Battle of Gettysburg

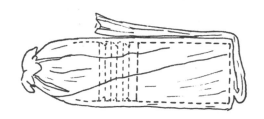

by
Dean S. Thomas

edited, with an Introduction by
Stephen V. Ash

drawings by
Andy Rice

photographs by
Dean S. Thomas

Copyright © 1981, 1993, 2007 Dean S. Thomas

Published by THOMAS PUBLICATIONS
3245 Fairfield Road
Gettysburg, PA 17325

Printed in the United States of America

ISBN-0-939631-00-8

TABLE OF CONTENTS

ACKNOWLEDGEMENTS

A number of individuals assisted me in making this book what it is, but responsibility for its shortcomings is mine alone. I would like to express my sincere thanks, to Stephen V. Ash, who took a rather cumbersome manuscript, shaped it into its final readable form, and also wrote the Introduction; to Andy Rice for his excellent line drawings created from some oftentimes crude sketches that I had supplied him; to William A. Frassanito, who made available photographs of the "wounded" trees in Part V; to Michael Musick, Archivist, Old Army and Navy Branch, National Archives and Records Service, who greatly assisted with the location of records and documents in the Archives; and to the following individuals who supplied information, specimens to photograph, or otherwise encouraged me to undertake this project: Al Flickinger, Corky Huey, Paul Klatt, Wendell Lang, Lewis Leigh, George Lower, Paul Miller, Ron Shealer, Bill Smith, and Chuck Thompson. To those I have omitted — my sincere apologies.

Dean S. Thomas
February 1981

INTRODUCTION

In the spring of 1863 General Robert E. Lee's Army of Northern Virginia stood poised to invade the North and, with luck, crush its adversary — the Army of the Potomac — in one climactic battle, ending the Civil War and establishing Confederate independence. Lee did not take this gamble lightly: the stakes were high, but so was his confidence in his gray-clad soldiers, fresh from victory at Chancellorsville.

Beginning in early June, Lee's divisions slipped away one by one from their positions near Fredericksburg, Virginia, moved northwest to the Shenandoah Valley, and then northeast into Maryland and Pennsylvania. Having carried the war at last to the heart of the enemy's country, the Confederate troops reveled in the abundance of the Pennsylvania farmland and provisioned themselves generously from it. But Lee was concerned with his primary task — finding and defeating the Union army — and grew more anxious each day he failed to hear from his cavalry commander, General "Jeb" Stuart, charged with scouting the enemy.

That enemy had not been idle. Under a new commander, George G. Meade, the Army of the Potomac had cautiously moved northward as Lee's intentions became clear, always staying between the Confederates and Washington, DC. On the evening of June 30, Union cavalry troopers bumped into a detachment of Lee's infantry near Gettysburg, in south-central Pennsylvania.

Lee had not planned to fight at Gettysburg, but he decided at once to make this his opportunity and on July 1 ordered his scattered divisions to converge on the town. Luck was with the Confederates that day. Though the Federal cavalry and their infantry reinforcements from the I Corps and XI Corps put up a stiff fight west and north of town, they were eventually outflanked on their right and left by Confederate infantry under A.P. Hill and R.S. Ewell, which drove the Yankee troops in some confusion back to Cemetery Hill just south of the town.

Overnight both armies rested and brought up reinforcements, and Meade made the critical decision to stay and fight where he was. On July 2 Lee again assaulted both Union flanks, but with mixed success. On the Confederate right, fresh troops under James A. Longstreet drove the poorly positioned Union III Corps back through a peach orchard, a wheatfield, and a low rocky hill known as Devil's Den, only to be rebuffed by the determined stand of some Federal V Corps regiments on Little Round Top, a large hill several miles south of Gettysburg. That evening, Ewell, on the left, attacked a brigade of the Union XII Corps dug in on Culp's Hill, just southeast of Cemetery Hill, but without decisive result.

On July 3 Lee decided (over Longstreet's vehement objections) to attack the center of the Union line, convinced that it had been weakened to reinforce the flanks. A force of about 12,000 Confederate infantrymen, with General George Pickett's division of Virginians as its nucleus, marched across a mile of open ground at three o'clock that afternoon and rushed the Union line. But that line was strong, its blue-coated II Corps defenders unflinching, and "Pickett's Charge" smashed futilely against it. As the survivors straggled back to the Confederate lines, Union cavalry east of town stopped Jeb Stuart's attempt to get behind the northern army.

Lee acknowledged his responsibility for the disaster and began planning his retreat back to Virginia. He would never again invade the North, never again come this close to victory. The Battle of Gettysburg, at a cost of over 10,000 American lives, had ended the Confederate dream of nationhood.

Stephen V. Ash
Knoxville, Tenn.

Map (opposite) of the Gettysburg battlefield showing the relative positions held by the various Union corps and Confederate divisions during the different stages of the battle. Adapted from G.K. Warren's "Map of the Battle-field of Gettysburg." Atlas to Accompany Official Records of the Union and Confederate Armies – 1861-1865.

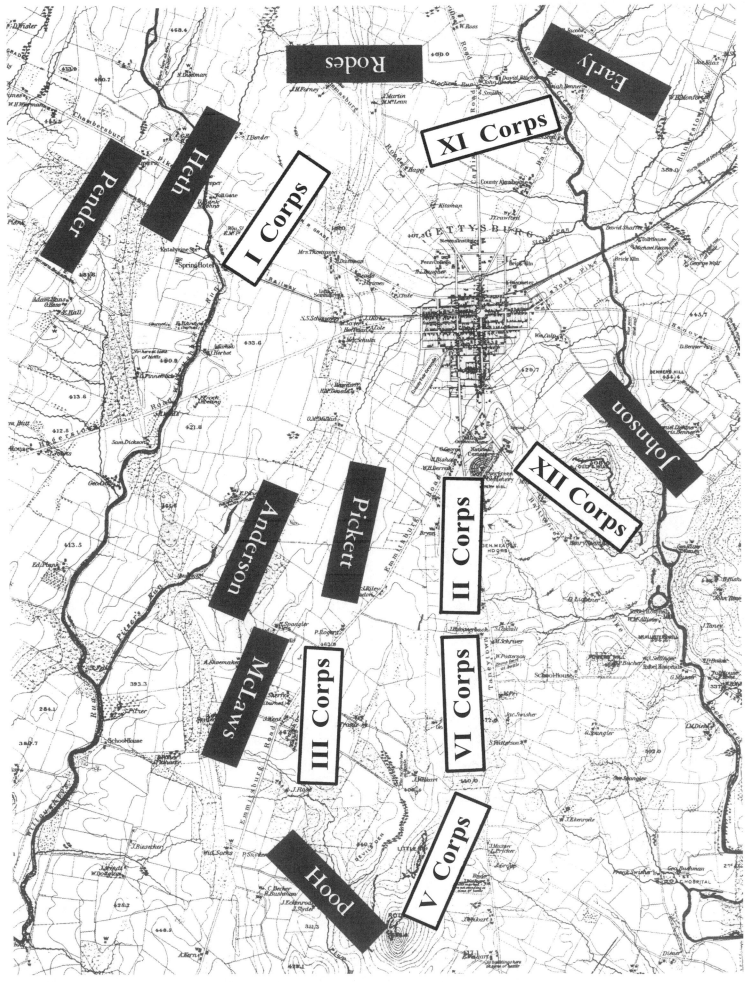

PART I: THE SYSTEMS OF FIREARMS

The visitor to Gettysburg is often amazed to see the large numbers of lead missiles and other paraphernalia of war that have been recovered from the battlefield. These items are housed in many fine museums in the area. A little more than a casual glance over these collections reveals that a great variety of artifacts exists. Cartridge boxes are of different sizes, buttons have varied motifs, belt plates have "US's" and "CS's," and bullets have many assorted forms. It is the intention here not only to describe these various bullets that are peculiar to the Battle of Gettysburg, but also to give the reader an appreciation of the reasons for this diversity. Before we "tour" the battlefield and look at what the soldiers left behind, let us briefly discuss some definitions and the six general categories of small arms projectiles and systems of firearms.

Ball, bullet or projectile is used here to mean the same thing — that which is fired from a small arm (pistol, carbine, rifle or musket). A cartridge is properly the bullet, powder, and casing combined to make a complete round of ammunition.[1] The cartridge case or wrapper may consist of paper, copper, skin or other materials. (The white residue or patina that forms on bullets after they have been exposed to a corrosive for some time is lead oxide.[2]) Three ringed, elongated bullets are those projectiles that are most commonly encountered. Technically, the rings or grooves are called cannelures and were employed to hold a lubricant or anti-fouling agent, although it was thought by some that they also helped increase accuracy. The 3-ringer is often termed a "minnie ball" — but please note that it is *not round*! "Minnie" is derived from the name of the French officer, Captain Claude Minié, who is credited with designing this projectile; however, the final form was more a product of the fertile mind of James H. Burton, Master Armorer at the Harpers Ferry Armory in the mid-1850s.

The six general categories of Civil War bullets and the weapons that fired them are explained and depicted below:

1) **Smoothbore** — The bore (inside diameter of the barrel) is not rifled, but is smooth. The projectile generally employed was a spherical ball or round shot. Since all Civil War military smoothbore weapons were muzzleloaders, it was necessary to put the bullet down the barrel before it could be shot out. Allowing for some degree of fouling (black powder residue build-up on the bore), the ball had to be of a smaller diameter than the actual diameter of the bore. This space between the bullet and the barrel is called windage. Because of the windage in smoothbores the ball does not take a true or straight path as it travels through and exits from the barrel, but tends instead to bounce from side to side and take an erratic course when it leaves. Smoothbores were very inaccurate at ranges over 50 yards and were useless over 100 yards.

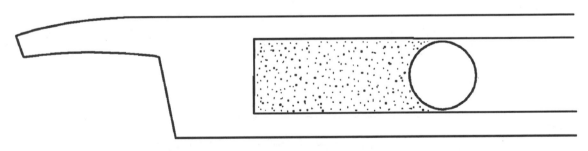

1) View of the breech of a smoothbore weapon loaded with a spherical ball.

2) **First Rifles/American System** — Rifling, the cutting of grooves into a gun barrel, and its improvement of accuracy has been practiced for some time. As early as 1500 the Germans had experimented with rifles; however, they were extremely cumbersome and had a very slow rate of fire. In order for a bullet to take the rifling, virtually all of the windage must be "destroyed." This was accomplished in the first rifles by merely using a ball of the same diameter as the bore, and forcing it down the barrel by means of a ramrod and mallet. The process was quite time consuming, and this prevented the general military adoption of rifles until the early 1800s when several more workable systems were invented.

3) **"Uniform Disfiguration of the Ball"** — During the early 1800s several European countries led by France evaluated methods of facilitating the loading process of rifles and destroying windage. This system encompasses those in which the bullet is of a smaller diameter than the bore and is expanded into the rifling by means of the ramrod and an anvil in the breech. The term "uniform disfiguration" refers to the regulated change of form that the ball undergoes *before* the powder charge ignition.

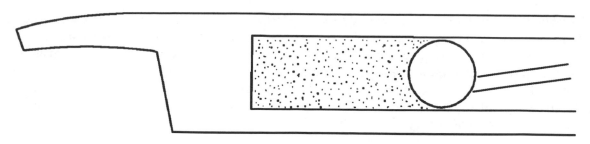

2) The breech of an early rifle loaded with an unpatched round shot.

Since few of the weapons and projectiles of this system saw use in this country, the different methods will be merely highlighted:

A. M. Delvigne of France developed a gun with a raised shoulder or rim projecting above the bottom or breech of the bore. This chamber held the powder and provided the anvil upon which the ball was rammed. The windage allowed the ball to enter the bore freely and position itself in the center of the barrel. With three blows of the rammer the lead was driven into the rifling and the windage disappeared.

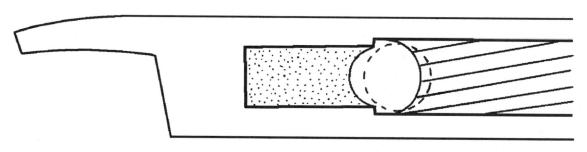

3) A. The System of Delvigne. The spherical ball is shown rested on the raised shoulder (dotted line)
and in its rammed position (solid line).

B. M. Pontchara of France added a patched wooden sabot to the ball. This was to prevent the ball from being driven into the chamber during ramming.

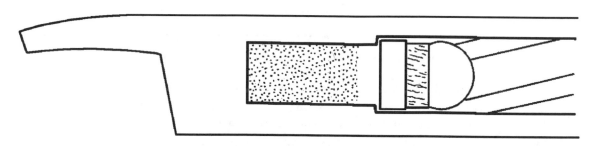

3) B. Pontchara's development — a ball with a patched wooden sabot.

C. M. Augustin of Austria eliminated Pontchara's sabot and beveled the inside edge of the shoulder to assure, he felt, the correct positioning of the ball in the center of the bore.
D. M. Thouvenin of France was not satisfied with the above methods and devised an iron stem or "tige" placed in the center of the breech. The tige, like the shoulder, acted as an anvil upon which the ball was expanded by the ramrod.

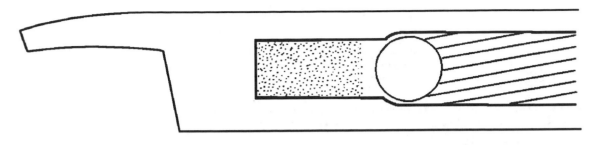

3) C. The breech of a rifle with a beveled shoulder as designed by Augustin.

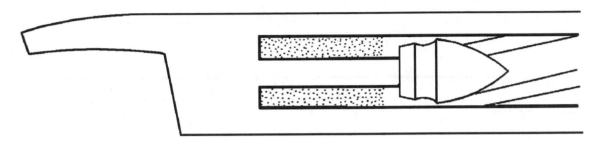

3) D. The system of Thouvenin. An elongated ball with a solid base rests on the stem.

E.   The work of Delvigne, M. Tamisier, and Claude Minié improved on the projectiles for the tige weapons, but their work eventually led to the development of an entirely new system.

4) **"Normal Form of the Ball"** — In this system the bullet, of smaller diameter than the bore, is preserved in its shape during the loading process. Then it is expanded (or "upset") by the action of the powder gases, to destroy the windage and take the rifling. The majority of projectiles fired from muzzleloaders during the Civil War employed this system; however, they accomplished their expansion in slightly different ways:

A.   The original bullet conceived by Captain Minié in 1849, was cylindro-conical (a cylinder topped by a cone) with three grooves or cannelures. A truncated cone cavity in the ball was closed at the base by a sheet iron cup. The windage allowed the bullet to drop easily down the barrel. In operation the powder charge explosion forced the iron cup toward the nose of the ball and at the same time the cup expanded the walls of the projectile into the rifling of the weapon.

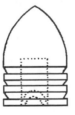

4) a. Captain Minié's ball with the sheet iron cup in the cavity.

B.   Bullets that used aids to expansion such as the sheet iron cup or a wooden plug remained in use throughout the Civil War years, notably in the English Enfield. However, in America during the mid-1850s experiments conducted at Harpers Ferry and Springfield Armories revealed that the cup or plug was unnecessary to expand the ball; the powder gases acting in a cone shaped cavity were alone enough to expand the bullet into the rifling.

C.   The English Wilkinson bullet is also of this system, although this projectile has a solid, flat base and two grooves. Here the action of the powder forces the thin edges of the sides of the grooves into the rifling before propelling the entire bullet out the barrel.

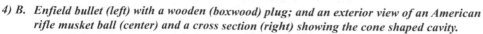
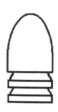

4) B. Enfield bullet (left) with a wooden (boxwood) plug; and an exterior view of an American
rifle musket ball (center) and a cross section (right) showing the cone shaped cavity.

4) C. Wilkinson bullet.

5) **"Fitted"** — This system is similar to that of the "Normal Form of the Ball" in that the shape of the bullet is preserved during loading; however, its operation is not dependent on the expansion of the ball. Here the bullet is the same shape as the bore, but of slightly smaller diameter. These weapons are not rifled in the usual sense of the word, but present a path for the bullet to follow. The windage is such that through careful loading the projectile can be forced easily to the breech. Although time consuming, this tight "fit" gave far greater accuracy with certain models than weapons of other systems.

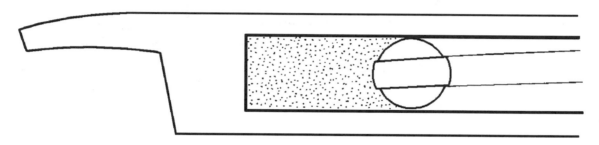

5) The breech of a Brunswick rifle. The "belt" around the ball corresponds with two spiral grooves in the barrel.
Jacobs and Whitworth rifles are also of this system.

6) **Breechloading** — The sixth and final category, and the principle upon which "modern" weapons are designed, is the breechloading system. Here the bullet is inserted from the rear or breech of the weapon. Unlike the other systems, the ball does not have to be expanded by a ramrod or by the action of the powder in order to take the rifling. Nor does the bullet follow a manufactured path, even though the "fitted" weapons could be made to load from the rear. The essence of breechloading is that the bullet and powder, or complete cartridge, is held in a separate chamber at the breech of the barrel. The bullet is made slightly larger than the diameter of the bore. When the powder charge is ignited the bullet is driven forward until it meets the rifled bore, and there it is compressed and elongated and forced to take the rifling.

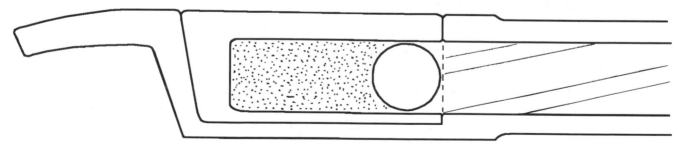

6) View of the chamber of a breechloader loaded with loose powder and a round ball.

This system had been experimented with for years before the Civil War, with resulting improvements in ease of loading and destruction of windage; however, the system initially had its drawbacks. The main problem was not overcome until improvements were made in metallic cartridge cases, and until that time few breechloaders saw military service. During the Civil War, breechloading rifles, carbines, and revolvers were used with varying degrees of success.[3]

PART II: THE MANUFACTURE OF BULLETS AND SMALL ARMS AMMUNITION

Civil War bullets were manufactured in several different ways. The most elementary of these was casting, i.e., pouring molten lead into a mould made of iron or brass. Moulds contained one or more cavities and are categorized by the location from which the lead is poured into the cavity and forms the bullet, viz.: nose cast, side cast, lip cast, or base cast.

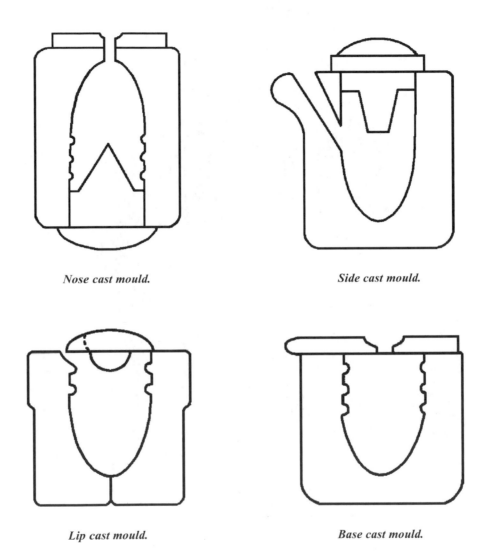

Nose cast mould.   *Side cast mould.*

Lip cast mould.   *Base cast mould.*

Casting was the least satisfactory method of forming a bullet. It required that the lead and mould both be extremely hot to prevent layering and air bubble entrapment which impaired the accurate flight of the bullet. After the ball was cast the excess lead or sprue had to be removed. Often the sprue removal was done as an integral operation of the mould while the bullet was still in the cavity. If not, the bullet was taken from the mould and trimmed by separate means.

Prior to the introduction of the elongated expanding ball into the United States service, round balls had been made at several U.S. arsenals by machines using pressure or compression. "Balls thus made are more uniform in size and weight, smoother, more solid, and give more accurate results, than cast balls."[4] In 1854, with the adoption by the U.S. Army of the "minnie" ball, a machine for their production was ordered to be constructed at the Allegheny Arsenal in Pittsburgh.[5] By 1863 at least one of these or similar machines was in operation at the Benicia, Calif., Frankford (Philadelphia), St. Louis, Washington, Watervliet, N.Y., and Allegheny arsenals.[6] To operate them the lead was first cast into round cylindrical bars and then rolled to a length of twenty-five inches. These bars were then fed to the machine which cut off a part sufficient for one ball and transferred it to a die in which the ball was formed, with cavity and rings. The die was in two pieces, similar to a mould, and was operated by cams. A punch formed the cavity in the base of the bullet and at the same time forced the slug of lead into all the crevices of the die, the surplus metal being forced out in a thin belt around the ball in the direction of the axis. The die opened, the bullet dropped out, the die again closed and was ready to receive the next slug of lead. The balls were trimmed by hand, with a knife, and were then passed through a gauge of the proper size.[7]

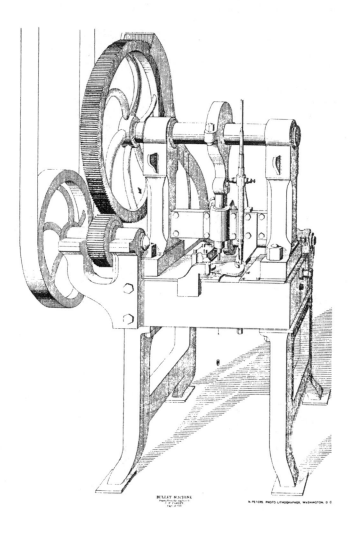

Bullet machine of the type in use at several Federal arsenals.
The lead bar is shown protruding from the slender hollow shaft
a little to the right of center. **Ordnance Memoranda No. 8.**

An English variation of the above method, for the manufacture of the Enfield bullet, involved the use of a one piece die and two punches. One punch, with a conical indentation, actually became a part of the die and formed a portion of the nose of the bullet during compression. The other punch acted, as in the American method, to form the ball with its cavity in the base. After the second punch was withdrawn, the first pushed the bullet out of the die in the direction in which the second had exited, then returned to its prior position.[8]

Another method of bullet manufacture was "pressed and turned." These machines took a lead slug and pressed it to form the nose and cavity. The partially formed ball was then transported to an automatic lathe where a cutting tool formed the grooves and finished the bullet as it spun. A machine of this type was put in operation at Frankford Arsenal in 1862.[9]

Generally speaking, small arms cartridges for Civil War muzzleloading weapons consisted of a rolled paper cylinder tied with string at the bullet end. This contained the projectile and a second smaller paper cylinder with the appropriate powder charge. A series of folds closed the open end. Ten cartridges were bundled in a paper wrapper along with twelve percussion caps and tied with string. One hundred bundles were crated in a wooden box and stenciling identified the contents. (Descriptions of various patented carbine and revolver cartridges, as well as Confederate ammunition, will be found below.) Cartridges used by the Union forces at Gettysburg could

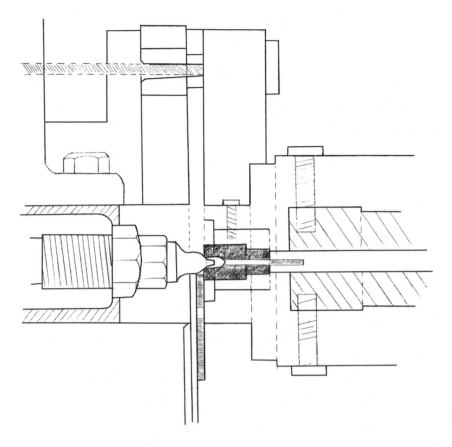

View of a portion of an English bullet machine.
Lead wire enters from the upper left, a slug is cut off, and transferred to the die
at center. Both punches are in their compressed positions. **Rifle Ammunition.**

have been made at any of the following United States arsenals, although it is doubtful if any from Benicia were shipped so far east. (Many cartridges were also made by private firms, not listed here.):

1) Allegheny
2) Benicia
3) Frankford
4) St. Louis
5) Washington
6) Watertown (Massachusetts)
7) Watervliet
8) Columbus (Ohio State Laboratory)
9) Indianapolis (Indiana State Arsenal)

Watertown and Columbus did not manufacture bullets, but were supplied by private firms and other arsenals. Eighteen private companies supplemented the bullet requirements of the U.S. Ordnance Department.[10]

Unfortunately, less is known about Confederate ammunition production. The Army of Northern Virginia may have carried products of these facilities to Gettysburg:

1) Atlanta Arsenal
2) Augusta Arsenal (Georgia)
3) Charleston Arsenal (South Carolina)
4) Columbus Arsenal (Georgia)
5) Fayetteville Arsenal (North Carolina)
6) Lynchburg Ordnance Depot (Virginia)
7) Macon Arsenal (Georgia)

8) N.C. Institute, D.D. & B. (Raleigh, N.C.)
9) Richmond Laboratory
10) Savannah Ordnance Depot
11) Selma Arsenal (Alabama)

However, since Richmond was the largest fabricator of small arms ammunition in the South[11] and the Confederacy lacked adequate transportation facilities, it is probably safe to assume that most of the cartridges in Lee's ordnance wagons were from Fayetteville, Lynchburg, and Richmond, supplemented by imported English ammunition and captured Federal ammunition.

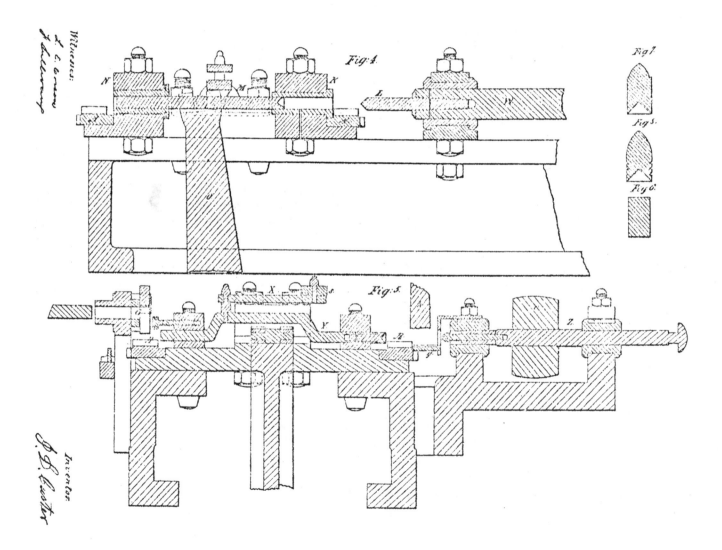

Two views of the bullet machine patented by J.D. Custer of Norristown, Pa. The "pressing" takes place in the center of Fig. 4. The bullet is "turned" at the left of Fig. 5. Fig. 6 shows the raw slug of lead, Fig. 7 the partially formed ball, and Fig. 8 the finished bullet. Letters Patent No. 43,102, June 14, 1864.

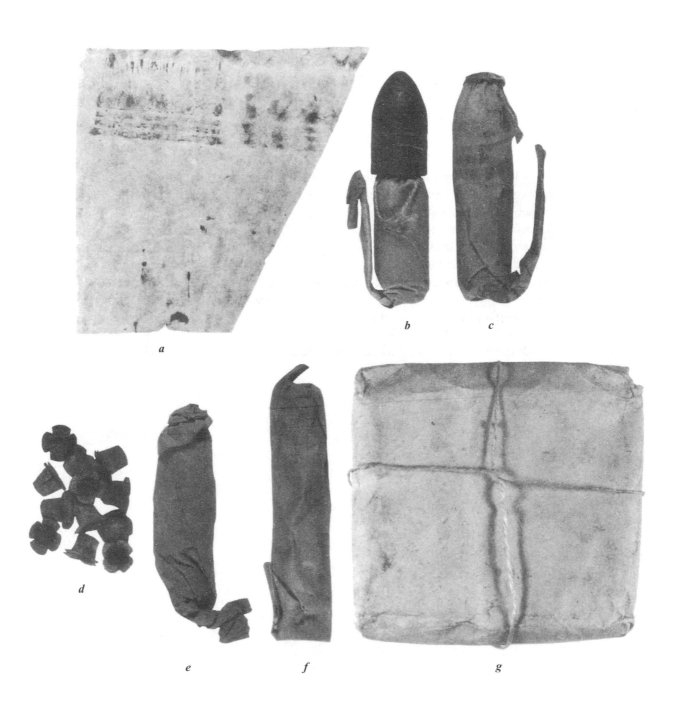

a. Outer, paper cartridge wrapper from b. (not to scale); b. .58 cal. rifle musket bullet with powder cylinder; c. complete .58 cal. rifle musket cartridge; d. percussion caps were charged with a small amount of fulminate of mercury; they ignited the powder charge of Civil War percussion firearms; e. and f. paper wrapped packages of twelve percussion caps each; and g. paper wrapper contained ten .58 cal. rifle musket cartridges and one package of twelve percussion caps.

The bullet specimens depicted on the following pages were actually recovered in the Gettysburg area or are the same type as those seen in local museums and collections. No attempt has been made to illustrate every die and mould variation, but the basic bullet types are all shown. In some cases discretion must be used in proclaiming a bullet to have been employed by one unit and not another since more than one body of troops traversed certain sections of the battlefield. The Union bullets have been grouped by corps and the Confederate bullets by divisions. Generally, these larger army units attacked or defended their own well defined portions of the battlefield. This broad categorization should compensate for "contamination" of areas caused by the intermixing of smaller units within the corps and divisions.

PART III: THE ARMY OF THE POTOMAC

The Union Army of the Potomac, commanded by Major General George Gordon Meade, marched to Gettysburg with about two-thirds of its 72,000 infantrymen[12] armed with either .58 cal. Springfield or .577 cal. Enfield rifle muskets. The remainder carried .54 cal. Austrian or U.S. rifle muskets, assorted .577 or .58 cal. foreign rifle muskets, .69 cal. rifled muskets, and at least eight regiments had .69 cal. smoothbore muskets. A few companies had breechloaders.[13]

The .58 cal., 3-ringer minnie ball or rifle musket bullet known officially as an elongated ball, was the projectile predominantly employed by the Yankees in both the Springfield and the Enfield. This is, therefore, the most frequently encountered bullet in the Gettysburg area. Generally speaking, the bullet weighed 500 grains (about one and one-eighth ounces), and was about one inch long, with an outside diameter of .574 inch, a pointed nose, cone shaped cavity, and three rings or cannelures to hold grease.

As mentioned earlier, the United States adopted the minnie ball, with modifications and refinements, in the mid-1850s. Numerous variations of these bullets, reflecting different methods and locations of manufacture, are encountered among those found at Gettysburg.

Unfortunately, no consolidated reports of small arms ammunition usage or expenditure are given for the Battle of Gettysburg in the *Official Records*. In fact, only three Union reports mention this information at all.[14] Nevertheless, these reports and other facts do give us a hint as to what occurred.

A circular dated June 30, 1863, issued by the headquarters of the Army of the Potomac, directed that:

> ...Corps commanders will hold their commands at readiness at a moment's notice, and, upon receiving orders to march against the enemy, their trains (ammunition wagons excepted) must be parked in the rear of the place of concentration. Ammunition wagons and ambulances will alone be permitted to accompany the troops. The men must be provided with three days' rations in haversacks, and with 60 rounds of ammunition in the boxes and upon the person....[15]

Theoretically then, the Union infantry was marching to Gettysburg with 4,320,000 (72,000 x 60) rounds of small arms ammunition "in the boxes and upon the person."[16] (The cartridge box held forty rounds, so twenty went in haversacks, knapsacks, or pockets, or were discarded.) The ammunition wagons carried at least this amount, but exact numbers are not known.[17] Assuming another eighty to ninety rounds per man in the ammunition wagons, this placed an additional 5,760,000 to 6,480,000 rounds on the battlefield. That the initial 4,320,000 was expended (fired, lost, or dropped in the heat of battle, or just thrown away) is shown by another circular dated July 5, 1863:

> The major general commanding enjoins it upon all corps commanders to be very careful in (expending) their ammunition, both artillery and infantry.
>
> We are now drawing upon our reserve trains, and it is of the highest importance that no ammunition be exhausted unless there is reason to believe that its use will produce a decided effect upon the enemy.[18]

Brig. General John W. Geary's report, alluded to above, states that his command (Second Division, XII Corps) of approximately 3,700 enlisted men "expended in the fight on July 3, and in subsequent skirmishing, 277,000 rounds of ammunition.[19] This represents about seventy-five rounds per man and apparently does not include expenditures by one of the division's brigades on the evening of July 2.

Additional evidence in this regard is offered by Lt. J.G. Rosengarten, Ordnance Officer, I Corps. Although he stated his tabulation of 228,000 rounds was the amount of small arms ammunition "expended," his method of presentation leads one to believe that these were the additional quantities of cartridges issued from the wagon trains to the troops.[20] If this last assumption is correct then the I Corps of 8,700 men,[21] expended about eighty-six rounds per man in the battle (sixty rounds carried to the field and twenty-six issued from the trains).

It can be ascertained from two other reports that the original allotment of sixty rounds of ammunition was used up. Brig. Gen. John C. Robinson, Second Division, I Corps reported that "No soldiers ever fought better, or inflicted severer blows upon the enemy. When out of ammunition, their boxes were replenished from those of their killed and wounded comrades."[22] Col. Joshua L. Chamberlain commanding the 20th Maine Infantry, Third Brigade, First Division, V Corps stated that his men were not so particular about where they found ammunition: "The intervals of the struggle [he wrote] were seized to gather ammunition from the cartridge-boxes of the disabled friend or foe on the field.... We opened on them as well as we could with our scanty ammunition snatched from the field.... My ammunition was soon exhausted...."[23]

Obviously, all this shows only that a few units used more than sixty rounds per man. Some must have expended less. Col. Hiram Berdan, commanding the 1st and 2nd U.S. Sharpshooters, reported that "We went into action with about 450 rifles. During the three days, we expended 14,400 rounds of ammunition."[24] — or, only thirty-two rounds per man. The VI Corps with 13,500 men saw little action, so expenditures must have been small. Nevertheless, the other units of the Army of the Potomac were hotly engaged at different times during the battle like elements of the I, V, and XII Corps described above. In one form or another (fired or dropped), expenditures of small arms ammunition by the infantry of the Army of the Potomac (including the VI Corps) on the battlefield at Gettysburg must have equaled at least seventy-five rounds per man or a total of 5,400,000. This is the equivalent of about 193 tons of lead and twenty-three tons of black powder.

A.   I Corps

The I Corps was the first body of Union infantry to arrive on the battlefield. It replaced the Federal cavalry troopers in the fields west and northwest of the town during the morning of July 1.

Lt. J.G. Rosengarten's report, mentioned earlier, states that the following calibers of small arms ammunition were issued: .54, .57, .58, and .69.

| 1 | 2 | 3 |

1 & 2   .54 cal. for rifles and rifle muskets. These smaller versions of the .58 cal. 3-ring minnie ball were also adopted in the mid-1850s. Intended originally for the U.S. model .54 cal. rifles, during the Civil War they were used with those and foreign rifle muskets (particularly Austrian) of .54 to .55 cal.

3   .54 cal. rifle musket cartridge.

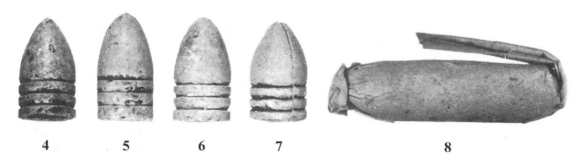

| 4 | 5 | 6 | 7 | 8 |

4 – 7   .58 cal. for rifle muskets. These bullets were of such dimensions that they could be and were used in both .577 cal. Enfield rifle muskets and .58 cal. Springfield rifle muskets,[25] although the wooden ammunition boxes sometimes specified that their contents were intended only for Enfields. Illustrated are the stencilings from three boxes.

8   .58 cal. rifle musket cartridge.

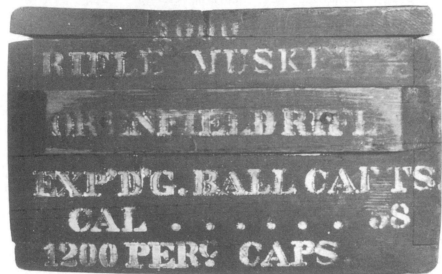

End views of ammunition boxes for 1000 rifle musket cartridges.

| 9 | 10 | 11 | 12 | 13 |

9 & 10   .58 cal. for rifle musket with "star" in the base cavity. The star was formed by an engraved punch during the pressing operation. Most of these projectiles are of similar dimensions though the size of the star may vary. There is no agreement among experts as to who manufactured these bullets.

Star in base, base view.

11   .58 cal. for rifle muskets, "pressed and turned." The manufacture of these bullets was described in Part II. The marks in the cavity were formed by the center that revolved the ball during the "turning" operation. Although more than one patent was issued for machinery that pressed and turned bullets, this projectile may be a specimen of the type produced at the Frankford Arsenal.

Pressed and turned, base view.

12   .58 cal. for rifle muskets, Williams patent Type I. This bullet was designed by Elijah D. Williams of Philadelphia and secured by Letters Patent No. 35,273 on May 13, 1862. The projectile was cast with the projecting "pin" as an integral part of the body. Two concavo-convex (having one concave side and one convex side) zinc discs with six slits were placed on the pin which was peened to hold them in place. Originally intended to increase accuracy in rifle muskets, the flattening of the zinc discs by the powder charge explosion "evidently keeps that part of the barrel through which it passes free from foul and lead."[26] The initial order for bullets was placed in December, 1861,[27] and they were supplied to the Federal arsenals to be made up into cartridges.

Williams Type I, cross section.

13   .58 cal. Williams patent Type I rifle musket cartridge. These cartridges were fabricated in the same manner as the regulation .58's, and with the same powder charge. For identification they were often wrapped in other than the standard buff-colored paper, viz: blue or red. Originally, when adopted, one Williams cartridge was bundled with nine regulation .58's;[28] however, by April 1863, the ratio was ordered increased to three Williams and seven regulation cartridges.[29]

14   .69 cal. spherical ball for smoothbore muskets (commonly called a round ball or round shot). These projectiles were relics from a bygone era, but the need for serviceable weapons during the Civil War dictated their use in the .69 cal. smoothbores. Most spherical balls manufactured by the Federal government were pressed, but private manufacturers supplied some cast balls.

15   .69 cal. round shot cartridge.

16   .69 cal. for rifled muskets. (See Part III, Section D below.)

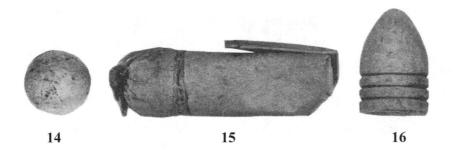

14   15   16

B.   II Corps

On July 3 the II Corps held the center of the Union position on Cemetery Ridge and bore the brunt of "Pickett's Charge." The previous day portions of the corps had reinforced both the left and right of the sagging Federal line.

No II Corps officers reported on small arms ammunition consumed or issued, but this corps appears to have had only slightly more variety in its ammunition than the I Corps.

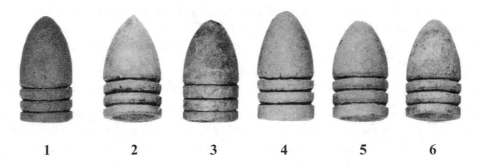

1   2   3   4   5   6

1   .54 cal. for rifles and rifle muskets.

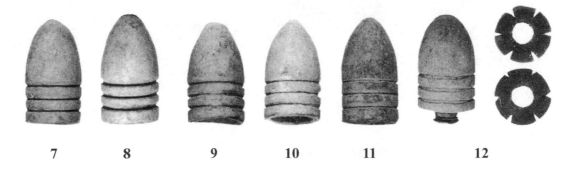

7   8   9   10   11   12

2 – 8   .58 cal. for rifle muskets. Seven variations are depicted.

9   .58 cal. for rifle muskets with a star in the base of the cavity.

10   .58 cal. for rifle muskets with "US" in the base of the cavity. Similar to those with the star in the base, here, too, the marking was formed by an engraved punch during pressing. Although the fabricator is not known, the "US's" and "stars" may have been produced at the same locality.

11   .58 cal. for rifle muskets, "pressed and turned."

12   .58 cal for rifle muskets, Williams patent Type I. Specimen is without the two zinc discs, which are shown separate.

US in base, base view.

23

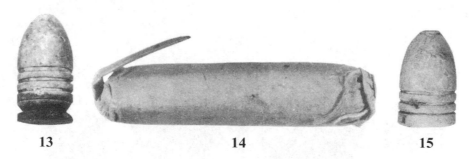

13   14   15

*Williams Type II,
cross section.*

13   .58 cal. for rifle muskets, Williams patent Type II. Modifications made by Williams to his Type I projectile led him to secure Patent No. 37,145 on December 9, 1862. Although both the Type I and II consisted of three pieces, the Type II was quite different in appearance and construction. The pin of the Type II was cast of hardened lead as a separate piece and was "headed." Only one zinc disc, without slits, was held by the pin. The nose cast bullet body contained a small cavity into which the pin was placed, partially filling the cavity. In operation, the powder gases drove the pin forward into the body, flattening the zinc disc and expanding the bullet into the rifling. Williams claimed that "extremely accurate shooting is thus produced."[30] The flattened zinc discs of both the Type I and II scraped away the fouling in the bore as they exited from the gun, hence the nickname "cleaner" bullets. It is interesting to note, however, that in neither Patent No. 35,273 nor No. 37,145 does Williams mention this feature. Nevertheless, the Federal government by its testing became well aware of the benefit.

14   .58 cal. Williams patent Type II rifle musket cartridge. The paper of this specimen has a yellow tinge.

15   .58 cal. for rifle muskets, Williams regulation. This projectile is "the regulation bullet [3-ring, .58 cal. with cavity] made by the proprietors of the Williams bullet. The bullet is cast in moulds of peculiar construction."[31] The similarities between this ball and the Williams Type II are obvious.

16   17   18   19

16   .69 cal. round shot for smoothbore muskets.

17 & 18   .69 cal. Buck & Ball for smoothbore muskets. Civil War Buck & Ball consisted of one .69 cal. round shot surmounted by three .31 cal. buckshot, intended to increase the chances of hitting a target when fired from a highly inaccurate smoothbore musket. However, some soldiers were not content with these still slim odds — Col. William E. Potter of the 12th N.J. Infantry described the scene on July 3 as his men awaited Pickett's advance:

> ...[T]he regiment was armed with the Springfield smoothbore musket, calibre 69 — a terrible weapon at close range. The usual cartridge carried a large ball and three buckshot, but many of the men, while awaiting the enemy's advance, had opened their boxes and prepared special cartridges from ten to twenty-five buckshot alone....[32]

Specimen #17 shows the ball and three buckshot separated, while #18 shows the four pieces fused.

19   .69 cal. Buck & Ball cartridge.

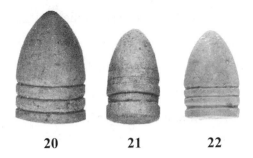

20

21

22

20   .69 cal. for rifled muskets. (See Part III, Section D below.)

21   .52 cal. for Sharps breechloading carbine or rifle. In the II Corps, portions of the 14th Connecticut Infantry, 1st Company of Massachusetts Sharpshooters, and 1st Minnesota Infantry had Sharps rifles at Gettysburg. (See Part III, Section C below.)

22   .54 cal. for Merrill breechloading rifle. The 1st Company of Massachusetts Sharpshooters had some of these weapons. (See Part III, Section H below for a photograph of a Merrill carbine cartridge. The rifle cartridge was probably similar, but may have contained a larger powder charge.)

C.   III Corps

The collapse of the III Corps line on the afternoon of July 2 put the army in jeopardy. The Corps had advanced without orders and left the vital position of Little Round Top unprotected.

The III Corps appears to have used the largest variety of ammunition of any corps in the Army of the Potomac; however, here again, there are no reported issuances or consumptions, with the exception of Col. Hiram Berdan's report of the 1st and 2nd U.S. Sharpshooters.

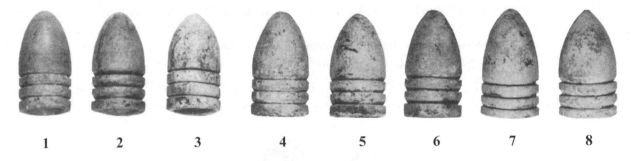

1   **2**   **3**   **4**   **5**   **6**   **7**   **8**

1 – 3   .54 cal for rifle muskets — three variants. A large proportion of the ammunition left behind by the III Corps was of this caliber. Specimen #3 is an example of a "pressed and turned" ball of a type other than that already described.

4 – 8   .58 cal. for rifle muskets — five variants.

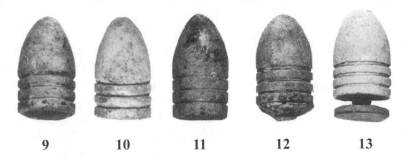

9   **10**   **11**   **12**   **13**

9	.58 cal. for rifle muskets with star in the base of the cavity.
10	.58 cal. for rifle muskets with "US" in the base of the cavity.
11	.58 cal. for rifle muskets, "pressed and turned."
12	.58 cal. for rifle muskets, Williams patent Type I.
13	.58 cal. for rifle muskets, Williams patent Type II.

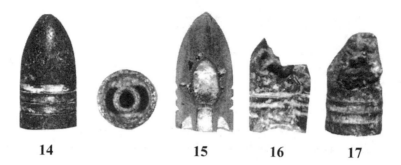

14   **15**   **16**   **17**

14   .58 cal. for rifle muskets, Gardiner patent explosive "Musket Shell." Samuel Gardiner, Jr., of New York City was awarded Patent No. 40,468 for this unusual projectile on Nov. 23, 1863. The U.S. War Department tested this bullet in the spring on 1862, and prior to the Battle of Gettysburg a total of 110,000, in two calibers,[33] were purchased.

> ...[T]he shell is in the shape the same as an elongated rifled bullet, and is provided with a cavity made of a hollow copper sphere around which the metal of the shell is pressed. The shell is arranged with a time fuze in the butt that communicates the flame to the bursting charge....[34]

Because the Gardiner was cast of pewter (an alloy of tin with lead, brass or copper, and more brittle than pure lead) it exploded into several ragged fragments. It was thought that these fragments would wound, the small explosions would create confusion, and "that shots properly directed to the caissons of the enemy will in exploding set fire to and blow them up."[35] Well preserved specimens have the fine raised lettering "S. Gardiner's Shell Patent Secured" on the base rim.

16 & 17   Two exploded specimens of the .58 cal. Gardiner patent explosive "Musket Shell." The 2nd New Hampshire Infantry of the III Corps carried approximately 14,000 of these bullets to Gettysburg.[36]

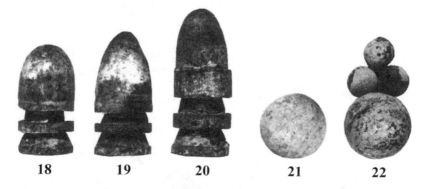

18   **19**   **20**   **21**   **22**

18 – 20   .58 cal. for rifle muskets, Shaler patent "Sectional" bullet. The three commonly encountered types are illustrated. Patent No. 36,197, dated August 12, 1862 was granted to Reuben and Ira W. Shaler for this "Improvement in Compound Bullets for Small-Arms." The projectile was normally composed of three pieces nested together. In theory the three sections separated upon leaving the musket and the top section was supposed to be nearly as accurate as a standard minnie ball. The inventor insisted that "amid the smoke and confusion of battle it would possess a three-fold advantage over the 'Minie' ball. I am sure that it makes one man equal to three."[37] A mere 300,000 of these projectiles were purchased by the Federal government during the Civil War.[38] Apparently, this unusual projectile did not live up to the hopes of its inventors.

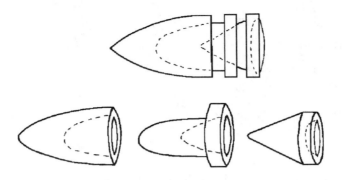

Shalers separated and complete; taken from a drawing sent by Ira Shaler
to Chief of Ordnance Ripley on October 9, 1861 (NARS).

21   .69 cal. round shot for smoothbore muskets.

22   .69 cal. Buck & Ball for smoothbore muskets.

23   .52 cal. for Sharps breechloading carbine or rifle. These "New Model" bullets replaced the old "ring-tail" ball about 1859. The Sharps projectiles were made either by casting or pressing — several variations are encountered. The 1st and 2nd U.S. Sharpshooters, and a portion of the 2nd New Hampshire Infantry had Sharps rifles in the III Corps at Gettysburg.

24 & 25 .52 cal. Sharps breechloading carbine or rifle cartridges. Specimens shown are the patented Johnton & Dow variety, and with linen case closed by a piece of thin paper. Several Federal arsenals and four private firms were manufacturing these cartridges prior to July 1863.[39] (See Part III, Section H below.)

D.   V Corps

On the afternoon of July 2 the bulk of the V Corps reinforced the III Corps but, more importantly, a portion of the V Corps saved Little Round Top.

The V Corps ammunition included many of the common types that we have already viewed, but contained a large number of .69 cal. rifled musket balls. This corps had more .69 cal. rifled muskets than any other corps in the Army of the Potomac.

1 – 6   .58 cal. for rifle muskets — six variants.

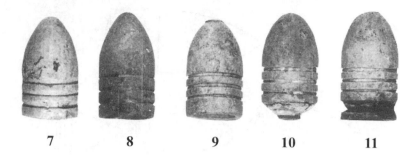

7	**8**	**9**	**10**	**11**

7 .58 cal. for rifle muskets with star in the base of the cavity.

8 .58 cal. for rifle muskets, "pressed and turned."

9 .58 cal. for rifle muskets, Williams regulation.

10 .58 cal. for rifle muskets, Williams patent Type I.

11 .58 cal. for rifle muskets, Williams patent Type II.

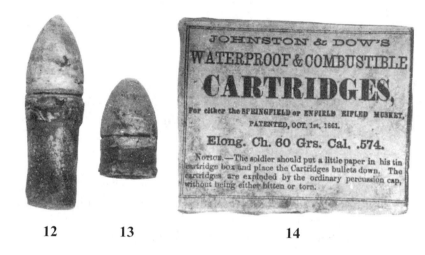

12	**13**	**14**

12 .577 or .58 cal. rifle musket cartridge by Johnston & Dow. The manufacture of these cartridges was protected by several U.S. patents. See Part III, Section H below for a description of these rounds.

13 .577 or .58 cal. for rifle muskets, Johnston & Dow. Bullets were supplied by the Federal government to Johnson & Dow to be made up into cartridges.

14 Cardboard box for 10 Johnston & Dow "Waterproof & Combustible Cartridges."

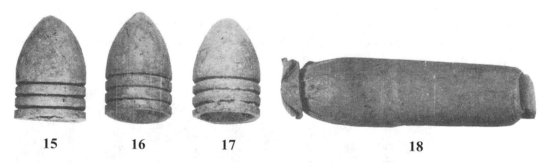

15	**16**	**17**	**18**

15 – 17 .69 cal. for rifled muskets. There are major variations in the size and shape of the cavities: left to right, cone cavity, small truncated cone cavity, large truncated cone cavity. These projectiles, like the .54's and .58's, were adopted by the United States in the mid-1850s. They were intended for rifled conversions of .69 cal. smoothbores as well as foreign .69 cal. rifled muskets.

18 .69 cal. rifled musket cartridge.

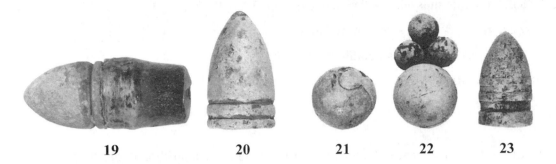

19   **20**   **21**   **22**   **23**

19   .69 cal. rifled musket cartridge, Elam O. Potter patent. Letters Patent No. 35,919 was issued for this round to Potter, of New York City, on July 22, 1862. The cartridge consisted of a compressed powder cake covered with collodion (nitrated cellulose dissolved in a mixture of alcohol and ether) and attached to the ball by a belt of collodion. Potter also manufactured cartridges of other calibers.

20   .69 cal. for rifled muskets. There is no agreement on the identity of this bullet. With the exception of two grooves versus three grooves, this ball is similar to the .54 cal. specimen #3 shown in the III Corps section above.

21   .69 cal. round shot for smoothbore muskets.

22   .69 cal. Buck & Ball for smoothbore muskets.

23   .52 cal. for Sharps breechloading carbine or rifle. The 13th Pennsylvania Reserves (Bucktails) had some Sharps rifles.

E.   VI Corps

The VI Corps marched thirty-five miles to the battlefield on July 2, but took part in little action.

Ammunition recovered from VI Corps areas shows much uniformity, but the variety of bullets carried by this corps was probably more extensive than depicted here. Many VI Corps units were sent as reserves to different sections of the Federal line, thus "contaminating" those sections of the field.

1   **2**   **3**   **4**   **5**   **6**

1 & 2   .54 cal. for rifle muskets.

3 – 7   .58 cal. for rifle muskets — five variants.

7   **8**   **9**   **10**   **11**

8	.58 cal. for rifle muskets, Williams patent Type I.
9	.69 cal. round shot for smoothbore muskets.
10	.69 cal. Buck & Ball for smoothbore muskets.
11	.69 cal. for rifled muskets.

F. XI Corps

The XI Corps arrived soon after the I Corps on July 1 and held a position in the fields north of Gettysburg for a short time before being routed. On July 2 its line was again broken temporarily on East Cemetery Hill.

The only reference to ammunition usage by the XI Corps is a statement by Lt. Rosengarten of the I Corps that he issued 13,000 rounds of .54 cal. ammunition from his trains to the Third Division of the XI Corps.[40] Nevertheless, the recovered XI Corps ammunition bears similarities to that used by the rest of the Army.

1	.54 cal. for rifle muskets.
2 – 5	.58 cal. for rifle muskets — four variants.
6 & 7	.58 cal. for rifle muskets with star in the base of the cavity, dropped and fired specimens.

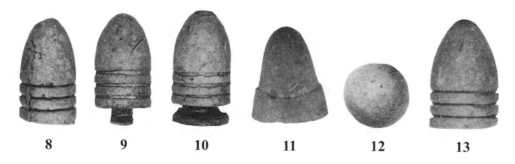

8	.58 cal. for rifle muskets with "US" in the base of the cavity.
9	.58 cal. for rifle muskets, Williams patent Type I.
10	.58 cal. for rifle muskets, Williams patent Type II.
11	.58 cal for rifle muskets, Shaler patent, section. Although this piece was located in an XI Corps area, it is not conclusive proof that any soldiers of that corps were issued these rounds. Similarly, Gardiner explosive bullets have been found in other than III Corps positions.
12	.69 cal. round shot for smoothbore muskets.
13	.69 cal. for rifled muskets.

F. XII Corps

From the night of July 1 until the close of the battle, the XII Corps anchored the right of the army in the Culp's Hill area; however, when Confederates attacked the hill on the evening of July 2, most of the XII Corps had already been removed to support the III Corps. On the morning of July 3 the returning XII Corps counterattacked and re-secured the hill.

As mentioned earlier, Geary's division claimed to have expended 277,000 rounds. Standard .58 cal. bullets seem to have made up the bulk of the XII Corps' ammunition, but notably large quantities of Williams Type I projectiles have been encountered in this corps' areas.

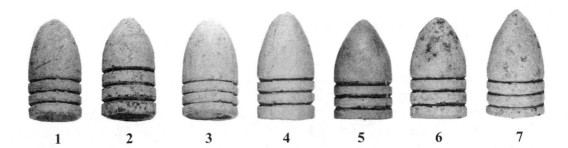

| 1 | 2 | 3 | 4 | 5 | 6 | 7 |

1	.54 cal. for rifle muskets.
2	.58 cal. for rifle muskets, "pressed and turned."
3 – 7	.58 cal. for rifle muskets — five variants.

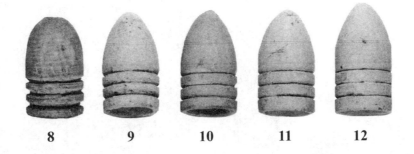

| 8 | 9 | 10 | 11 | 12 |

8	.58 cal. for rifle muskets. These bullets were nose cast and may not be of northern origin.
9	.58 cal. for rifle muskets with star in the base of the cavity.
10	.58 cal. for rifle muskets with "US" in the base of the cavity.
11 & 12	.58 cal. for rifle muskets, "pressed & turned," two variations.

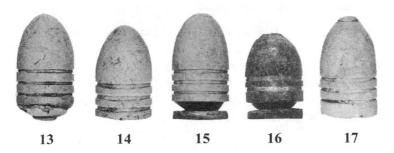

| 13 | 14 | 15 | 16 | 17 |

13 & 14	.58 cal. for rifle muskets, Williams patent Type I. Specimen #14 has had the washers removed and the pin cut off flush with the base. These bullets were once thought to have been intended for Gatling guns. (The Gatling guns were forerunners of the modern machine gun and were not used at Gettysburg.)
15	.58 cal. for rifle muskets, Williams patent Type II.

16   .58 cal. for rifle muskets, Williams patent Type III. These projectiles are shorter versions of the Type II and came into use sometime in 1863. They are very uncommon finds in sites occupied prior to 1864, but several alleged to have come from XII Corps areas at Gettysburg are known.

17   .58 cal. for rifle muskets, Williams regulation.

H. Cavalry Corps

Units of the Cavalry Corps took part in numerous small skirmishes in the Gettysburg vicinity. In particular, its stands west of the town on the morning of July 1 and southeast of town on the afternoon of July 3 were commendable.

The Army of the Potomac eventually brought about 13,000 cavalrymen to the Gettysburg area before the battle ended.[41] General Orders No. 30 (see Appendix 2) had specified the supply of ammunition to be kept on hand, "for cavalry, 100 rounds of carbine and 40 rounds pistol, with that in the cartridge-boxes." It is not known if the circular dated June 30 modified these quantities; at any rate, there are no recorded issues or expenditures of ammunition by the Union cavalry in the *Official Records*.

The Federal troopers at Gettysburg carried an assortment of carbines and rifles, but all were breechloaders. With the exception of two companies of the 6th Michigan and all of the 5th Michigan who were armed with Spencer repeating rifles,[42] all the cavalrymen had single-shot weapons.

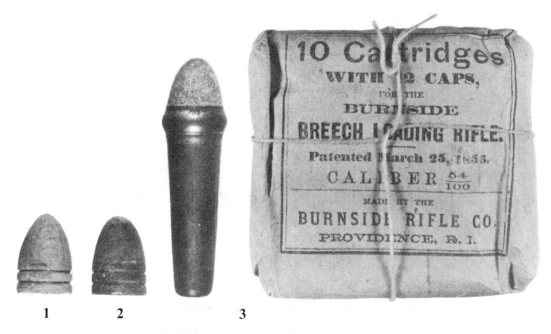

1   .54 cal. for Burnside carbine, flat base.

2   .54 cal. for Burnside carbine, dished base.

3   .54 cal. Burnside carbine cartridge and wrapper manufactured by the Burnside Rifle Co., Providence, R.I. The cartridge case with its swelled portion was patented by George P. Foster on April 10, 1860 (No. 27,791). The drawn brass case was charged with about 45 grains of powder and the bullet was crimped in place. A wad between the powder and ball prevented deterioration of the projectile. This is properly termed a "separate primed" round: the percussion cap flame ignited the powder charge through a perforation in the base of the case.

4   .50 cal. for Gallager carbine, common variety.

5   .50 cal. for Gallager carbine, variant with more pointed nose and six cuts or marks in the cavity.

6   .50 cal. Gallager carbine cartridge. These were supplied to the Federal government by Richardson and Overman of Philadelphia, but were actually manufactured by John Krider. After an April 1863 explosion at the Krider factory, Samuel Jackson continued the work.[43] Like the Burnside, the Gallager cartridge case was drawn from brass and the bullet was crimped into the case mouth. Ignition, too, was separate primed.

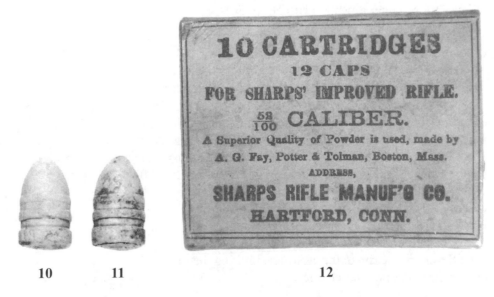

7 & 8   .54 cal. for Merrill carbine — two variations.

9   .54 cal. Merrill carbine cartridge and label from a box of cartridges. The Merrill cartridge consisted of a small piece of paper wrapped and pasted around the ball. After charging with 40 grains of powder the open end of the case was folded closed. The cartridge was loaded whole into the weapon and a percussion cap ignited the charge. Theoretically the entire paper case was consumed in the discharge.

10   .52 cal. for Sharps carbine or rifle. This variant was base cast and shows where the sprue was removed.

11   .52 cal. for Sharps carbine or rifle. This type was made by machine. The small cone cavity was a "center" for the punch during pressing.

12   Cardboard box for ten Sharps cartridges manufactured for the Sharps Rifle Manufacturing Company, Hartford, Conn. The case of linen (or paper) was rolled on a former and pasted. After it had dried a small, square piece of very thin paper was pushed through the case to one end and pasted also. A charge of sixty grains of powder was placed in the case, the bullet glued in, and the case was then "chocked" around the ball to make sure it was secure. The percussion cap flame penetrated the thin paper to ignite the charge. (See Part III, Section C, specimens #24 and #25 above.)

13   14   15

13   .50 cal. for Smith carbine — variation with raised band above the groove.

14   .50 cal. for Smith carbine — variation without the raised band above the groove.

15   .50 cal. Smith carbine cartridge and cardboard box for 10 cartridges as supplied by Poultney & Trimble, Baltimore, Md. Gilbert Smith of Buttermilk Falls, N.Y., the inventor of this carbine, was granted Patent No. 17,702 for this unusual cartridge on June 30, 1857. The cartridge case consisted of india-rubber cloth or vulcanized india-rubber that would expand in the chamber and seal the breech. The cartridge contained fifty grains of powder that received the flame from the percussion cap through a perforation at the base of the case.

16   .52 cal. for Spencer repeating rifle. (No. 56)

17   .52 cal. Spencer repeating rifle cartridge. The rimfire Spencer was one of the few "modern" cartridges used in the Battle of Gettysburg. Unlike any of the others that have been described, the Spencer was completely self-contained: it had together in one piece the primer, powder, ball, and case. These cartridges were made for the Spencer Repeating Rifle Company under Smith & Wesson's Patent No. 27,933 dated April 17, 1860. The cartridge cases went through at least eight steps in the forming process before they were ready to be charged with fulminate, which was "spun" into the outer recesses of the rim or annulus at the base of the case. A forty grain powder charge was inserted and the bullet was crimped into the open end of the case. In operation, the hammer of the rifle struck the rim of the cartridge, igniting the fulminate and, in turn, the powder charge.

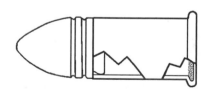

Spencer cartridge, cutaway view.

18   Cardboard box for forty-two Spencer cartridges manufactured by Crittenden & Tibballs of South Coventry, Conn. for the Spencer Repeating Rifle Co. The large box contained six smaller boxes of seven cartridges each.

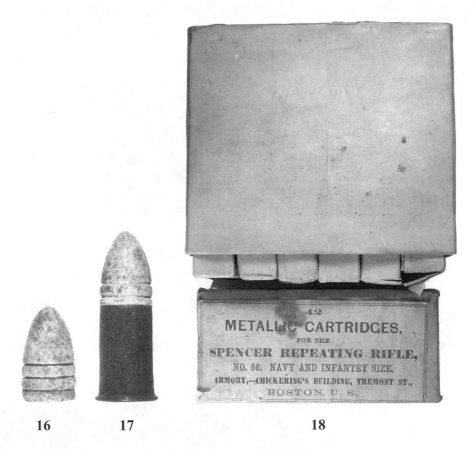

16   17   18

Revolvers carried by the cavalry included .36 and .44 cal. Colts and Remingtons, and others. Some of the ammunition shown may also have been used by infantry officers and artillerymen. All rounds described were separate primed and ignited by ordinary pistol percussion caps.

19   20   21   22   23

19   .36 cal. round ball for .36 cal. revolvers or pistols.

20   .44 cal. round ball for .44 cal. revolvers or pistols.

21   .44 cal. for Army revolver, Bartholow patent ("Army" revolver indicates .44 cal. size; "Navy" revolver indicates .36 cal. size).

22   .44 cal. Bartholow patent cartridge. This round was patented by Roberts Bartholow, a U.S. Army surgeon, on May 21, 1861. It consisted of a specially prepared powder cylinder, supposedly waterproof, which was glued to the ball; however, tests showed that the two parts often became separated. The illustrated specimen shows the silk strip that was eventually added by the manufacturer to reinforce the adhesion of the powder cylinder to the ball. Bartholow cartridges were also manufactured in other calibers.

23   Small blue colored box with label for six Bartholow "Army Holster Pistol" .44 cal. cartridges.

24   25   26

24   .36 cal. for Navy revolver, Colt.

25   .36 cal. Colt Navy cartridge by Colt Cartridge Works. The case was made of paper impregnated with saltpeter to ensure that it was entirely consumed.

26   Package for six .36 cal. Colt "Revolving Belt Pistol" cartridges. The outer wrapping label covers a split wooden block drilled to hold the six individual rounds.

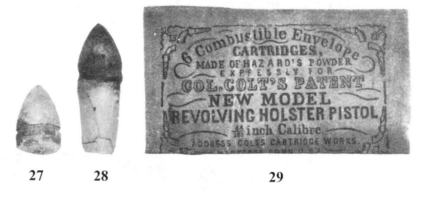

27   28   29

27   .44 cal. for Army revolver, Colt.

28   .44 cal. Colt Army cartridge by Colt Cartridge Works.

29   Package for six .44 cal. Colt "Revolving Holster Pistol" cartridges.

30   31   32   33   34

30   .36 cal. for Navy revolver, Hazard.

31   .36 cal. Navy cartridge made by the Hazard Powder Company under Doremus and Budd's patents of March 18 and March 25, 1862. The powder charge was compacted by pressure in a mould and, after being joined with the ball, the powder cylinder was coated with a waterproofing of shellac or collodion.

32   .44 cal. for Army revolver, Hazard.

33   .44 cal. Army cartridge, Hazard Powder Company.

34   Paper wrapper for six .44 cal. Hazard cartridges.

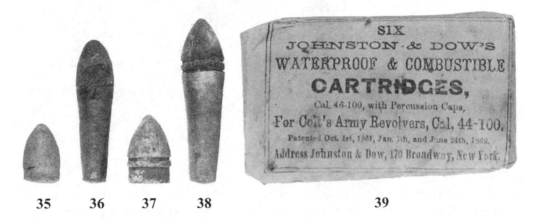

35   36   37   38   39

35   .36 cal. for Navy revolver, Johnston & Dow.

36   .36 cal. Navy cartridge by Johnston & Dow, New York City. These cartridges were manufactured under Johnston & Dow's patents of Oct. 1, 1861, and Jan. 7 and June 24, 1862. The cartridge case consisted of "treated paper, cloth or other fabric and was combined with powder and ball to make the cartridge perfectly combustible, entirely waterproof, and of great strength."[44]

37   .44 cal. for Army revolver, Johnston & Dow.

38   .44 cal. Army cartridge, Johnston & Dow.

39   Paper wrapper for six .44 cal. Johnston & Dow cartridges.

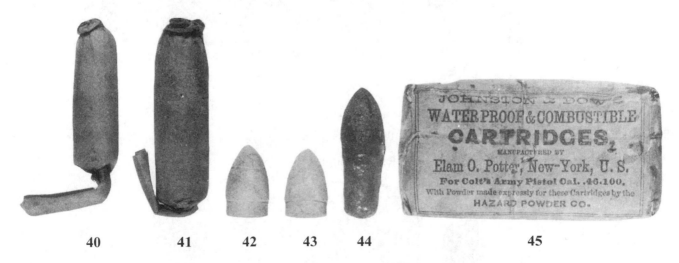

40   41   42   43   44   45

40   .36 cal. Navy cartridge, manufacturer unknown, but possibly the Frankford Arsenal. The cartridge contains a ball similar to specimen #35. The round is tied with twine above the nose of the bullet and has the usual fold found on larger caliber military ammunition.

41   .44 cal. Army cartridge, manufacturer unknown, but perhaps the Frankford Arsenal. This contains a ball similar to specimens #27 and #32.

42 & 43 .44 cal. for Army revolver, Elam O. Potter — two slight variations.

44 .44 cal. Army cartridge, Johnston & Dow, manufactured by Elam O. Potter.

45 Paper wrapper for .44 cal. Johnston & Dow cartridges by Elam O. Potter.

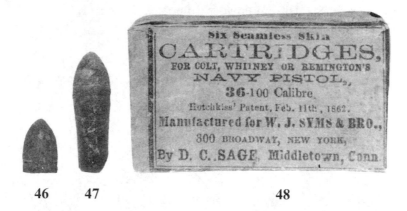

46 **47** **48**

46 .36 cal. for Navy revolver, Sage.

47 .36 cal. Navy cartridge, Sage "seamless," by D.C. Sage, Middletown, Conn. This was made under Julius Hotchkiss' patent No. 34,367 of Feb. 11, 1862, which called for strips of mutton or hog's gut to be spirally wound on a former to make a cartridge case. The case was then charged with powder and attached to the ball by a thread.

48 Package for six .36 cal. Sage seamless cartridges. The paper wrapping covers a drilled wooden block.

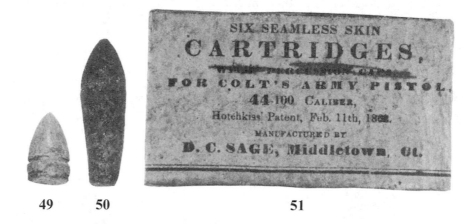

49 **50** **51**

49 .44 cal. for Army revolver, Sage.

50 .44 cal. Army cartridge, Sage "seamless," by D.C. Sage.

51 Package for six .44 cal., Sage seamless cartridges.

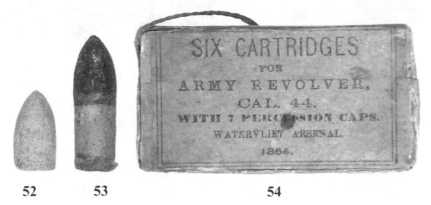

52 **53** **54**

52   .44 cal. for Army revolver, Watervliet Arsenal.

53   .44 cal. Army cartridge by Watervliet Arsenal. The cartridge case is formed of ordinary untreated paper and glue to the ball.

54   Cardboard box for six .44 cal. "Army Revolver" cartridges, Watervliet Arsenal. (Post-Gettysburg date.)

I.   Miscellaneous —Union

The following projectiles were used at Gettysburg but cannot be identified by corps.

1   **2**   **3**   **4**

1   .44 cal. cartridge for Ballard (New Model) carbine or rifle, rimfire ignition.

2   .52 cal. for Sharps & Hankins (First Model) carbine or rifle.

3   .52 cal. Sharps & Hankins (First Model) carbine or rifle cartridge, rimfire.

4   .54 cal. Gardiner explosive for .54 rifle musket or .52 cal. breechloader. Made in the pattern of a Sharps bullet but with the fuse nozzle extending about 1/8 inch beyond the base of the ball, 25,000 of these projectiles were ordered in December 1862.[45] These "shells" functioned like the larger .58's, but whether they were intended for sharpshooters or cavalry has not been determined. Nice specimens have the same lettering on the base rim as the .58 cal. size. Gettysburg appears to have been one of the few battlefields where these projectiles saw use.

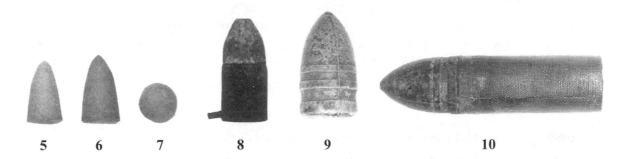

5   **6**   **7**   **8**   **9**   **10**

5 – 7   Pickets with round ball. These three bullets (along with others of the same kind) were found together. The name "picket" generally given to these conical shaped projectiles pre-dates the Civil War. Pickets were used in the famed Kentucky or Pennsylvania rifles, as well as in some sharpshooting or target rifles.

8   12mm. pin-fire for Lefaucheux and other pin-fire revolvers. Developed in France in the 1830s, the pin-fire saw limited use in the United States. Contained within the metallic cartridge case was a percussion compound resting on an anvil. When the hammer of the pistol struck the stout brass wire or "pin," the latter was driven into the percussion compound, exploding it and, in turn, the powder charge.

9   .56 cal. for Sharps breechloading rifle. Few Sharps rifles of this caliber were purchased by the Federal Ordnance Department, but several were used at Gettysburg.

10   .56 cal. Sharps rifle cartridge, linen case.

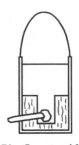

Pin-fire cartridge.

PART IV: THE ARMY OF NORTHERN VIRGINIA

Like its northern adversary, the Confederate Army of Northern Virginia commanded by General Robert E. Lee was armed chiefly with .577 cal. Enfield or .58 cal. Springfield type rifle muskets. In fact, the approximately 55,000 infantrymen[46] may have carried proportionately more of these weapons than the Army of the Potomac.[47] The balance of the Confederate small arms consisted of a wide variety of guns procured by domestic manufacture, foreign importation, and battlefield scavenging.

The most frequently encountered bullet at Gettysburg, of known Confederate origin, is the Gardner "insert." Its unique patented method of manufacture is described below. Gardners were made in .54, .58 (most common), and .69 calibers.

Even less is known about ammunition consumption at Gettysburg by the Southern troops than by the Army of the Potomac. No consolidated reports of Confederate small arms ammunition usage are reported in the *Official Records* and no orders have been located directing the quantities of cartridges to be carried north by Lee's soldiers or his supply wagons. Nevertheless, the fragmentary information available indicates that the Army of Northern Virginia was well provided with ammunition for its 1863 invasion. William LeRoy Broun, former Lieutenant Colonel of Ordnance and commander of the Richmond Arsenal, stated in 1888 that "never was an order received from General Lee's army for ammunition that it was not immediately supplied."[48]

Whatever Lee's wants in the late spring of 1863, they were at least partly supplied on June 14 by the capture of Winchester, Virginia. Union General Robert H. Milroy's division had abandoned at that place "about 200,000 rounds of small-arms ammunition."[49] Although Lee confirmed the capture of "a lot of ammunition"[50] by Richard S. Ewell's Corps, the exact fate of the 200,000 rounds cannot be determined. Perhaps they were carried to Gettysburg and used in the battle?

The analysis in Part III gave the number of cartridges that were supposed to have been carried to the battlefield by the Army of the Potomac, showed that some units "shot them all up," and then estimated the total expenditures. That was a simple task compared to the chore of drawing similar conclusions for the Army of Northern Virginia. It is known that many of the Southerners, too, "shot up" all of their cartridges, but unfortunately there is no pre-battle ammunition inventory[51] and the only post-battle inventory is a statement by Lee on July 10, 1863, that "the army is in good condition, and we have a good supply of ammunition."[52] To arrive at an estimate of expenditures, let us assume that the rounds fired per man were the same as determined for the Army of the Potomac — seventy-five. Fifty-five thousand infantrymen times seventy-five rounds per man equals 4,125,000 cartridges. That the army's ordnance officers performed well the difficult job of distributing this large quantity is indicated by Lee's tribute to them:

> The Chief of Ordnance and his assistants are entitled to praise for the care and watchfulness given to the ordnance trains and ammunition of the army, which, in a long march and in many conflicts, were always at hand and accessible to the troops.[53]

The notion that has persisted to this day that the Confederates were short of ammunition at Gettysburg should be put to rest.[54]

A. James Longstreet's First Corps — Lafayette McLaws's Division

On the afternoon of July 2, McLaws's Division crushed the Union III Corps salient at the Peach Orchard. Recovered bullet specimens indicate that the majority of the soldiers in McLaws's Division were armed with .577 or .58 cal. weapons. No reports in the *Official Records* give any hint about ammunition consumption for this unit.

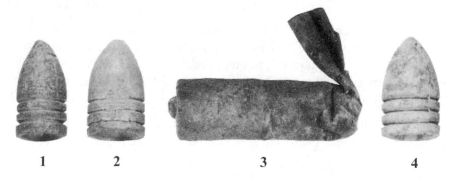

1   2   3   4

1   .54 cal. for rifles and rifle muskets. This bullet is of Confederate manufacture. It was nose cast and the sprue removed apparently by hand with a knife.

2   .58 cal. for rifle muskets. Nose cast in typical pre-Civil War federal bullet mould, probably made at the Lynchburg Ordnance Depot.

3   .58 cal. rifle musket cartridge containing a projectile like specimen #2. This is an unusual round in that the nose of the bullet is left exposed. The cartridge paper has been wrapped double for the length of the ball. After charging with powder, the open end was closed with the normal folds. This is an example of the "Spilman pattern" as made at the Lynchburg Ordnance Depot.

4   .58 cal. for rifle muskets. Of typical northern style, this ball may have been from captured Federal supplies brought to the battlefield, or perhaps was taken from a Union prisoner.

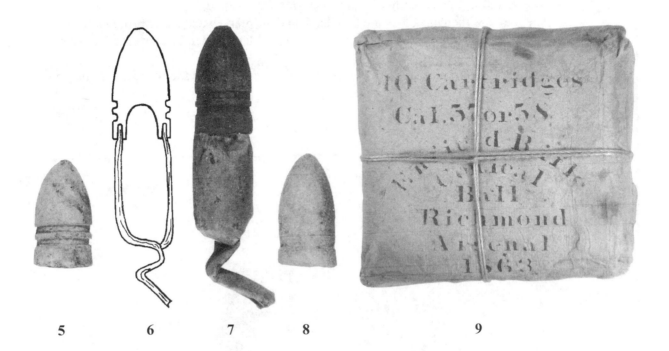

5   6   7   8   9

5   .58 cal. for rifle muskets, Gardner patent. C.S.A. patent No. 12 was issued to Frederick J. Gardner on Aug. 17, 1861, for this unusual projectile.[55] Unlike the "American" and English method of making paper cartridges where the ball was completely covered by paper, the bullet in a Gardner cartridge was entirely exposed. Gardner bullets were nose cast of lead with a large flange or ring perpendicular to the body of the bullet. To form a cartridge the bullet was inserted nose first into the base plate of a special machine. Cartridge paper was wound around a plunger directly above the bullet. A foot operated treadle moved the plunger with the paper down onto the bullet, and continued pressure drove the bullet through the base plate. This action crimped the paper into the bullet and also swaged the bullet to the proper size. The bullet with the paper cylinder attached was then filled with black powder and the "tail" folded closed in typical fashion. Ten cartridges with percussion caps were bundled in a paper wrapper and marked with the type of ammunition, place and date of manufacture. Gardner bullets and cartridges were made at the Augusta, Ga. and Charleston, S.C. arsenals; however, the majority were fabricated at the Richmond (Va.) Laboratory. (See Plate No. XXI.)

6   Drawing of a sectioned .58 cal. Gardner cartridge.

7   .58 cal. rifle musket cartridge, Gardner patent.

8   .58 cal. for rifle muskets, Gardner patent — variant mould cavity, very shallow grooves.

Plate No. XXI. Gardners method of attaching the paper cartridge to the Ball.

The object of this device was to expedite the manufacture of musket cartridges by superseding the necessity of tying the paper to the ball and at the same time swedge the ball to exact caliber and render the connection between it and the paper more accurate.

It is the invention of F.J. Gardner of N.C. and was used in the rebel arsenal at Richmond. The bullets were cast in the form shown in Fig. 1, having a circular flange, *a*, running around them immediately below the cannelures.

The paper was attached by turning down this flange upon the base of the ball, *c*, the paper, *g*, being caught between them as shown at, *e*, in Fig. 2. This was accomplished in a very simple manner in the machine shown in Fig. 3, 4, and 5.

The edge of the cartridge paper cut to proper size was inserted in the slot, *b*, of the steel plunger, *A*, and wound smoothly upon it by turning the handle, *B*.

The foot was then placed on the treadle, *T*, and the plunger and paper brought down on the bullet, *D*, forcing the latter through the swedging plate, *M*, the flange turned down and the paper caught.

Upon removing the foot from the treadle, the spring, *S*, lifts the plunger and the machine is ready to repeat the operation.

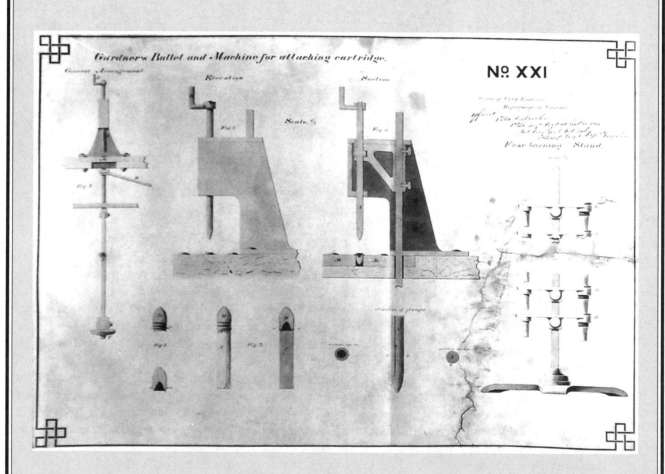

Lt. Michie's drawing No. XXI of "Gardner's Bullet and Machine for attaching cartridges"
also included a sketch of a "Fuse burning Stand."

9   Wrapper stenciled "10 Cartridges, Cal 57 or 58, Conical Ball, Richmond Arsenal, 1863." Typical of the Confederate Ordnance Department, cartridge packages were marked with the number and kind of cartridges and place and date of manufacture. Gardners of .58 cal. were intended for .577 or .58 cal. weapons.

10   **11**   **12**   **13**

10   .58 cal. for rifle muskets. Rarest of the three calibers of this "family" (.54, .58, .69). Manufactured in Raleigh, N.C.

11   .577 cal. for rifle muskets, Enfield pattern, nose cast–cone cavity. A bullet of this same general design known as the "Metford-Pritchett" was adopted by the British government in 1853 for use in the Enfield P/53 rifle musket. Although large quantities of Enfield ammunition were run through the blockade, this specimen was probably made by the Confederates in an imported or domestically made mould.

12   .577 cal. for rifle muskets, Enfield pattern, side cast–cone cavity. Variant of #11.

13   .577 cal. rifle musket cartridge, Enfield pattern ball, C.S. manufacture of typical "American" construction.

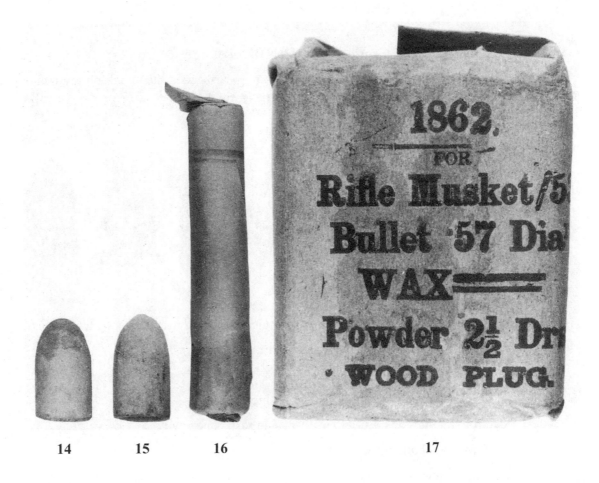

14   **15**   **16**   **17**

14 .577 cal. for rifle muskets, Enfield pattern, machine pressed–plug cavity with no marking, boxwood plug intact. In 1855 the English altered the cavity of the "Metford-Pritchett" ball and added an iron cup as an aid to expansion. The cup was later changed to a boxwood plug. This specimen was made in England and imported by the South.

15 .577 cal. for rifle muskets, Enfield pattern, machine pressed–plug cavity with "57" in the base. The "57" apparently stands for the caliber of the weapon or ball, and may have been used to check for worn forming punches. Of English manufacture, this specimen was made by Eley Bros. of London.

"57" in base, base view.

16 .577 cal. rifle musket cartridge, English Enfield pattern fabricated by Eley Bros. Unlike most period American cartridges, the English Enfield had the ball reversed (see drawing). The charge consisted of sixty-eight grains of powder.

17 Stenciled wrapper for ten Enfield cartridges. The British packaged their cartridges without percussion caps.

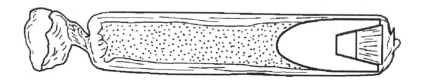

Enfield rifle musket cartridge of English manufacture.
Compared to American cartridges, the ball is reversed.

B. Longstreet's First Corps — George E. Pickett's Division

Pickett's Virginian's took part in no action until they spear-headed the attack on the Union center on the afternoon of July 3. They also appear to have been largely equipped with .577 or .58 cal. rifle muskets. No officers reported on ammunition expenditures.

1   2   3   4   5   6

1 .54 cal. for rifles or rifle muskets. This specimen may have been "lost" by a Yankee.

2 .58 cal. for rifle muskets, probably captured from Federals.

3 .58 cal. for rifle muskets, C.S. nose cast.

4 – 6 .58 cal. for rifle muskets, Gardner patent — three variations.

7 .577 cal. for rifle muskets, Enfield pattern, side cast–cone cavity.

8 .69 cal. for smoothbore muskets.

9   .69 cal. round shot cartridge attributed to Richmond Laboratory. Regulations called for the cartridge to contain 100 grains of powder.

7   8   9

C.   Longstreet's First Corps — John B. Hood's Division

Hood's Division struck the left of the Union III Corps on the afternoon of July 2, overran Devil's Den, and threatened Little Round Top before being halted. Of all Longstreet's divisions, Hood's appears to have had the largest assortment of bullets. Two of its regimental commanders reported consuming all of their cartridges. In describing his attack on the Round Tops, Lt. Col. L.H. Scruggs of the 4th Alabama stated: "We retired in good order, though not until we had expended our ammunition. Having received a fresh supply of cartridges about dark, we remained in the enemy's front, some 200 yards distant, during the night."[57] Lt. Col. P.A. Work of the 1st Texas noted that his men fired anything they could find:

> Having exhausted their original supply of ammunition, the men supplied themselves from the cartridge-boxes of their dead and disabled comrades and from the dead and wounded of the enemy, frequently going in front of the hill to secure a cartridge box.[58]

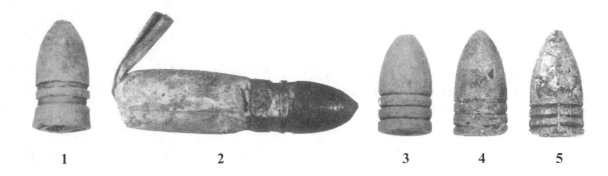

1   2   3   4   5

1   .54 cal. for rifles or rifle muskets, Gardner patent. This is the smallest of the three Gardner calibers.

2   .54 cal. rifle musket cartridge, Gardner patent.

3   .54 cal. for rifles and rifle muskets, probably of Yankee manufacture.

4 & 5   .54 cal. for rifles and rifle muskets, both probably of Confederate manufacture.

6   7   8   9   10   11

6	.54 cal. round shot for rifles, rifle muskets, or single shot pistols. This bullet was used in the M1841 "Mississippi" rifle and others before the introduction of the Minnie ball; however, by the time of the Civil War it was still employed widely by the Confederates.
7	.58 cal. for rifle muskets, probably Yankee.
8	.58 cal. for rifle muskets, possibly C.S. manufacture, crude cone cavity.
9 – 11	.58 cal. for rifle muskets, Gardner patent, three mould cavity variations.

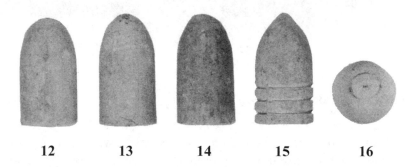

12   13   14   15   16

12	.577 cal. for rifle muskets, Enfield pattern, machine pressed, plug cavity with no marking.
13	.577 cal. for rifle muskets, Enfield pattern, machine pressed, plug cavity with "57" in the base.
14	.577 cal. for rifle muskets, Enfield pattern, machine pressed, plug cavity with "L" in the base. The "L" stands for E. & A. Ludlow, an English manufacturer of Enfield cartridges in Birmingham.

"L" in base.

15	.58 cal. for rifle muskets, "teat" cavity pattern. The method and location of manufacture of these bullets is as yet undetermined, but they are definitely Confederate.

"Teat" cavity, cross section.

16	.69 cal. round shot for smoothbore muskets, Confederate cast manufacture.

D.   Richard S. Ewell's Second Corps — Jubal A. Early's Division

Early's timely arrival from the northeast on the afternoon of July 1 helped to rout the Union XI Corps. On the evening of July 2 a portion of this division attacked East Cemetery Hill. Little variety is encountered in bullets found in the positions of Early's Division.

1	.54 cal. for rifles or rifle muskets, Gardner patent.
2 – 4	.58 cal. for rifle muskets, Gardner patent, three variations. Specimen #2 has been fired.
5	.577 cal. for rifle muskets, Enfield pattern, nose cast, cone cavity.
6	.577 cal. for rifle muskets, Enfield pattern, machine pressed, plug cavity with no marking.

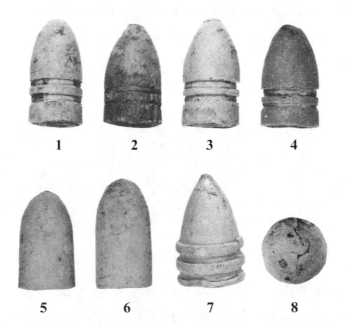

1 2 3 4

5 6 7 8

7   .69 cal. for rifled muskets, made in Raleigh, N.C., the largest of the three calibers (.54, .58, and .69) of this design. The 6th N.C. of Hoke's Brigade is known to have used these bullets in earlier campaigns.

8   .69 cal. round shot for smoothbore muskets, C.S. cast.

E.   Ewell's Second Corps — Edward Johnson's Division

Johnson's troops fought for possession of Culp's Hill on the evening of July 2 and the morning of July 3. Six officers of Johnson's Division reported exhausting their ammunition in the fight for Culp's Hill on July 3rd.[59] Capt. J.B. Golladay of the 33rd Virginia described the action:

> It is true that the supply of ammunition was exhausted after an hour or two of spirited fighting, but at the same time partial supplies were obtained upon the field, and thus part of the regiment was engaged for the length of time mentioned.
>
> The regiment was then withdrawn, and after it was gotten in some sort of order, replenished its exhausted stock of ammunition, &c., it was moved by the right flank, and, forming a line of battle several hundred yards to the right of the first position, advanced upon the enemy, and engaged him for half an hour or an hour.
>
> It was withdrawn from the position last named and marched to the rear, where it remained long enough to get some rest, and replenish once more its nearly exhausted ammunition.[60]

Quite a variety of bullet types was carried by Johnson's men, and particularly notable are the large quantities of Enfields.

1   2   3   4   5   6   7   8

1   .54 cal. for rifles and rifle muskets, Gardner patent.

2 & 3   .54 cal. for rifles or rifle muskets, Yankee manufacture.

4 & 5   .54 cal. for rifles or rifle muskets, probably C.S. manufacture.

6   .54 cal. for rifles or rifle muskets, Confederate nose cast.

7   .54 cal. for rifles. Confederates often referred to this conical ball as a "Harpers Ferry slug."

8 – 10   .58 cal. for rifle muskets, Gardner patent, three variations.

        9   10   11   12   13   14   15   16

11   .58 cal. for rifle muskets, probably C.S. manufacture.

12   .58 cal. for rifle muskets, nose cast(see Part III, Section G, specimen #8.)

13 – 16   .58 cal. for rifle muskets, C.S. nose cast, four variations.

        17   18   19   20   21   22   23   24

17   .58 cal. for rifle musket, "teat" base pattern.

18   .58 cal. for rifle musket, machine pressed and turned, five spokes in cavity. This was no doubt captured from Federals and carried to the battlefield.

19 – 22   .577 cal. for rifle muskets, Enfield pattern, four variations with cone cavities. Number 22 appears to have been machine pressed; the other three were cast.

23   .577 cal. for rifle musket, Enfield pattern, "teat" in cavity.

        25   26   27   28   29   30   31   32

24 – 27   .577 cal. for rifle muskets, Enfield pattern, machine pressed;
        #24: small plug cavity, no marking.
        #25: standard plug cavity, no marking.
        #26: plug cavity, marked "L."
        #27: plug cavity, marked "L^2."

"L^2" in base.

28	.69 cal. for rifled muskets.
29	.69 cal. round shot for smoothbore muskets.
30 & 31	.69 cal. for smoothbore muskets, long and short varieties of what were called "Nesler" bullets by the state of North Carolina. Made in Raleigh, N.C.
32	.69 cal. short "Nesler," fired specimen.

F. Ewell's Second Corps — Robert E. Rodes' Division

Rodes successfully attacked the right of the Union I Corps and the left of the Union XI Corps on the afternoon of July 1. Major Eugene Blackford, commanding the battalion of sharpshooters of the 5th Alabama, reported that "the average number of rounds fired was not less than 200,"[61] although this was certainly not typical of the rest of this division. Blackford also noted that "Abundant supplies of ammunition were obtained by sending details through the town to collect cartridge boxes."[62] Bullets used by Rodes' Division were common to the whole Army of Northern Virginia.

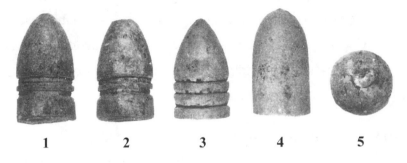

1 & 2	.58 cal. for rifle muskets, Gardner patent, two variations.
3	.58 cal. for rifle muskets, unknown origin, but probably Yankee.
4	.577 cal. for rifle muskets, Enfield pattern, plug cavity with no marking.
5	.69 cal. round shot for smoothbore muskets.

G. Ambrose P. Hill's Third Corps — Richard H. Anderson's Division

Anderson supported the left of McLaws's Division during the attacks on the afternoon of July 2 and nearly made a lodgement on Cemetery Ridge. On July 3 Anderson contributed to the failure of Pickett's attack by not properly supporting him on the right.

Like most in the army, the officers of Anderson's Division failed to mention ammunition supplies in their official reports. Recoveries indicate that this division was using many captured cartridges.

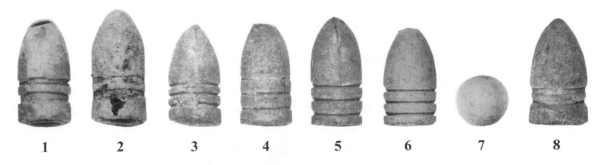

1 & 2	.54 cal. for rifles or rifle muskets, Gardner patent, two variations.
3	.54 cal. for rifles or rifle muskets, C.S. nose cast.
4	.54 cal. for rifles or rifle muskets, C.S. nose cast, crude variation.

5	.54 cal. for rifles or rifle muskets, "teat" base pattern.
6	.54 cal. for rifles or rifle muskets, Yankee manufacture.
7	.54 cal. round shot for rifles, rifle muskets, or single shot pistols.
8 & 9	.58 cal. for rifle muskets, Gardner patent, two variations.

10 – 12	.58 cal. for rifle muskets, three variations probably of northern manufacture.
13 & 14	.577 cal. for rifle muskets, Enfield pattern, two length variations with cone cavities.
15	.577 cal. for rifle muskets, Enfield pattern, plug cavity with no marking.
16	.69 cal. round shot for smoothbore muskets.

H. Hill's Third Corps — Henry Heth's Division

Heth's infantrymen opened the battle of Gettysburg on the morning of July 1 and, after a day of rest, took part in Pickett's disaster on July 3. Heth mentioned in his report that several of his regiments ran out of ammunition.[63] The 26th North Carolina collected some "from the enemy's dead, being entirely out themselves."[64] Heth's Division holds the distinction of having carried the largest variety of bullets to the battlefield of any Confederate division..

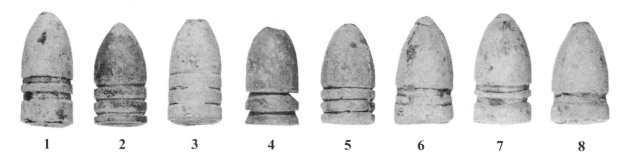

1	.54 cal. for rifles or rifle muskets, Gardner patent.
2	.54 cal. for rifles or rifle muskets, U.S. manufacture, plug cavity.
3	.54 cal. for rifles or rifle muskets, C.S. nose cast.
4	.54 cal. for rifles or rifle muskets, Wilkinson pattern. This bullet was designed in England in the 1850s (see Part I), but was a type adopted by the state of North Carolina and was made in Raleigh.
5	.54 cal. for rifles or rifle muskets, U.S. manufacture.
6 & 7	.58 cal. for rifle muskets, Gardner patent, two variations.
8	.58 cal. for rifle muskets or muzzleloading carbine, Gardner patent. The "one groove" variation weighs about 20% less than the common examples like #6 and #7.

| 9 | 10 | 11 | 12 | 13 | 14 | 15 | 16 |

9 .58 cal. for rifle muskets, C.S. "nose cap" variety.

10 & 11 .58 cal. for rifle muskets, two variations, probably removed from Yankee prisoners or dead.

12 .58 cal. for rifle muskets, French style with triangular-pyramid shaped cavity. This ball may have been imported by the South and appears to have been lip cast.

13 .58 cal. for rifle muskets, "New" Austrian, a Wilkinson type bullet developed in Austria for the Lorenz rifle. Like the Wilkinson, these balls were adopted by the state of North Carolina and cast in Raleigh.

14 – 16 .577 cal. for rifle muskets, Enfield pattern, three variations with cone cavities.

| 17 | 18 | 19 | 20 |

17 & 18 ..69 cal. for rifled muskets, two variations, U.S. or C.S. manufacture.

19 .69 cal. for rifled muskets, French style with triangular-pyramid shaped cavity. Projectiles of this design were developed in France in the late 1850s. This specimen was nose cast.

20 .69 cal. rifled musket cartridge, "triangular" cavity ball, French manufacture. The bullet is reversed like English ammunition.

Triangular-pyramid shaped cavity.

| 21 | 22 | 23 | 24 |

21 .69 cal. for rifled muskets, Gardner patent, shallow cavity type. This is the largest caliber of the Gardner patent bullets.

22	.69 cal. for rifled muskets, "teat" base pattern, the largest caliber of this type of bullet.
23 & 24	.69 cal. for smoothbore muskets, long and short varieties of the North Carolina "Nesler" bullets.

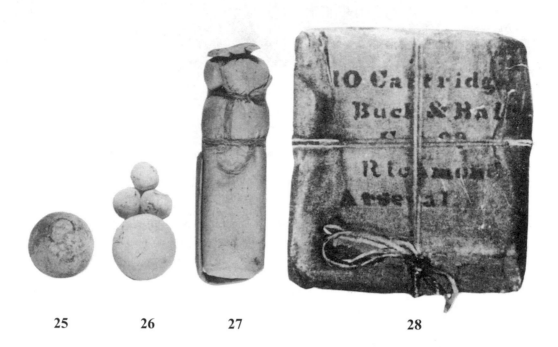

25	.69 cal. round shot for smoothbore muskets, C.S. cast.
26	.69 cal. for smoothbore muskets, Buck and Ball.
27	.69 cal. Buck and Ball cartridge, Richmond Laboratory. The cartridge contains 110 grains of powder.
28	Wrapper for ten Confederate Buck & Ball cartridges.

I. Hill's Third Corps — William D. Pender's Division

On the afternoon of July 1 Pender's Division helped complete the defeat of the Union I Corps, but remained inactive through the remainder of the battle. The men of Pender's Division carried typical Confederate ammunition to Gettysburg.

1 & 2	.54 cal. for rifles or rifle muskets, Gardner patent, two variations.
3	.54 cal. for rifles or rifle muskets, machine pressed and turned. These bullets are probably not of southern manufacture, but are often found in Confederate positions.
4	.54 cal. round shot for rifles, rifle muskets or single shot pistols.
5	.54 cal. round shot rifle cartridge, powder charge unknown.

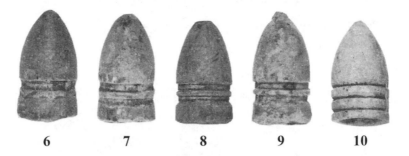

6	7	8	9	10

6 – 9   .58 cal. for rifle muskets, Gardner patent, four variations.

10   .58 cal. for rifle muskets, probably captured.

11	12	13	14	15	16

11 – 13   .577 cal. for rifle muskets, Enfield pattern, three variations, all with cone cavities.

14   .577 cal. for rifle muskets, Enfield pattern, very deep plug cavity with no marking.

15   .577 cal. for rifle muskets, Enfield pattern, plug cavity with "L."

16   .69 cal. round shot for smoothbore muskets.

J.   J.E.B. Stuart's Cavalry Division

Stuart's troopers had taken a circuitous route to Gettysburg and arrived there on the night of July 2. Their principle role in the battle was in the cavalry fight on July 3 in the fields east of town, involving about 6,000 southern cavalrymen.[65]

Stuart's cavalry was armed with a wide variety of small arms, including pistols, rifle muskets, muzzleloading carbines, and a few breechloading carbines. Stuart commented that by the time he reached Gettysburg, "My numerous skirmishes had greatly diminished — almost exhausted — my supply of ammunition."[66]

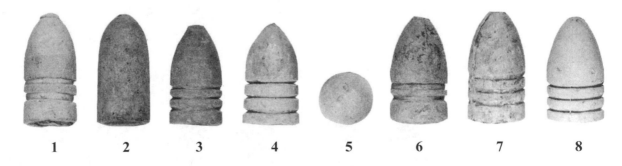

1	2	3	4	5	6	7	8

1   .54 cal. for rifles or rifle muskets, Gardner patent.

2   .54 cal. for rifles, rifle muskets, or carbines. Enfield-like ball without grooves, cone shaped cavity, of C.S. manufacture.

3   .54 cal. for rifles or rifle muskets, C.S. nose cast.

4   .54 cal. for rifles or rifle muskets, machine pressed and turned.

5   .54 cal. round shot for rifles, rifle muskets, or single shot pistols.

6   .58 cal. for rifle muskets, Gardner patent.

7   .58 cal. for rifle muskets, C.S. nose cast.

9   **10**   **11**   **12**   **13**   **14**

8 – 10   .58 cal. for rifle muskets, three variations, U.S. manufacture.

11   .577 cal. for rifle muskets, Enfield pattern, C.S. nose cast with cone cavity. A.G. Jenkin's brigade was largely armed with Enfield rifle muskets, but amazingly carried only ten rounds of ammunition per man to the battlefield.[67]

12   .69 cal. for smoothbore muskets, Buck and Ball.

13   .52 cal. for Sharps breechloading rifle or carbine. This bullet has what is commonly called a "ring-tail," but which more correctly should be termed a "tie" base ring or "tie" base groove. To form the cartridge, the cartridge paper was tied with twine to the ball at the deep base ring or groove. Though antiquated, this method of making Sharps cartridges was kept alive in the Confederacy. Captured Sharps rifles and carbines were used in the Confederate service, and by 1863 Sharps carbines of southern manufacture were available.

14   .52 cal. Sharps breechloading rifle or carbine cartridge. The cartridge paper was tied to the "ringtail" ball, charged with about sixty grains of powder, and the open end folded closed.

15   .54 cal. for Merrill breechloading carbine. This ball was made at the Richmond Laboratory for use in captured or pre-Civil War Merrill carbines.

16   .54 cal. Merrill breechloading carbine cartridge, Richmond Laboratory.

17 & 18   .50 cal. for unidentified breechloading carbine, C.S. cast, two slight variations.

19   .50 cal. for breechloading carbine, fired specimen.

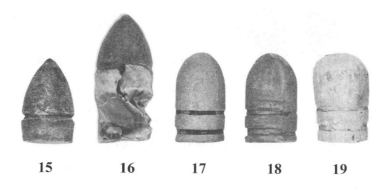

15   **16**   **17**   **18**   **19**

20   .36 cal. for revolvers, C.S. manufacture.

21   .36 cal. for revolvers, captured ammunition made by the northern firm of Johnston & Dow.

22   Packet of .36 cal. revolver cartridges. The paper covered, drilled wooden block is stenciled "6 cartridges Colt's Navy Pistol With Caps C.S. Laboratory Richmond, Va."

23   .44 cal. for revolvers, Colt Dragoon style.

24   .44 cal. for revolvers, Richmond Laboratory. This is similar in design to specimen #15 above.

25   .44 cal. revolver cartridge, Richmond Laboratory. Cartridge contains thirty grains of powder.

26   Packet of .44 cal. revolver cartridges. The paper covered, drilled wooden block is stenciled "6 Cartridges Colt's Army Pistol With Caps C.S. Laboratory Richmond, Va."

K.   Miscellaneous — Confederate

The following projectiles found at Gettysburg could not be associated with any particular Confederate division.

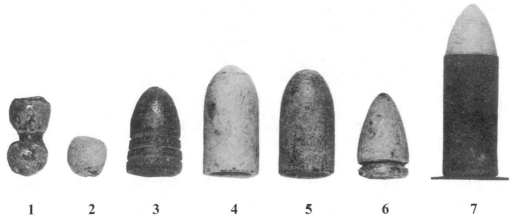

1   Approximately .44 cal. for single shot pistol. This projectile is commonly called a "bar-shot." It is presumably Confederate, or pre-Civil War non-military. The bullet was apparently cast in a crude stone mould and then cut in two.

2   Approximately .44 cal. for single shot pistol, one half of a "bar-shot."

3   .54 cal. for rifles or rifle muskets, plug-shaped cavity, fired specimen.

4   .577 cal. for rifle muskets, Enfield pattern, machine pressed with a dot in the base of the plug cavity.

Dot in base.   *"L¹" in base.*

5   .577 cal. for rifle muskets, Enfield pattern, machine pressed with "L¹" in the base of the plug cavity.

6   .50 cal. for Maynard carbine or rifle, pointed nose variety. Although considered northern weapons, many Maynards were purchased by southern states before hostilities began. It is possible, however, that this specimen was dropped by a post-Civil War hunter carrying a Maynard sporting rifle.

7   .50 cal. Maynard carbine or rifle cartridge. This features a brass cartridge case with a large brass disc (for extraction) soldered to the base. The percussion cap flame ignited the powder through a perforation in the base. The cartridge contained fifty grains of powder.

8   9

8   .45 cal. for English Whitworth or other target or sharpshooters rifles. No hexagonal Whitworth bullets are known to have been found at Gettysburg. Only the Confederates, as far as is known, imported Whitworth rifles during the Civil War. A Whitworth cylindrical bullet with an impressed "42" in the base cavity was found along the Confederate retreat route.

9   .45 cal. Whitworth rifle cartridge, English manufacture. The "tube" cartridge was patented in 1859. This specimen contained a powder charge of eighty-five grains.

10   11   12

10   Paper wrapped cardboard package for ten Whitworth cylindrical projectiles.

11   .54 cal. for rifles or rifle muskets, "teat" cavity pattern, variation.

12   .54 cal. for rifles or rifle muskets, the smallest caliber of this "family." Made in Raleigh, N.C.

PART V: **"THE AIR WAS ALIVE WITH SINGING, HISSING, AND ZIPPING BULLETS."[68]**

Relatively few bullets found their mark in a human target. Most plowed into trees, bounced off rocks, or fell harmlessly to the ground. The photographs in this section show some of the results of small arms fire.

1

1   Assorted fired bullets from the Gettysburg area.

2   3

2   A rarity — two bullets that collided in mid-air. Even with the tons of lead flying around, the odds that these two three-ringers would meet were extremely slim.

3   Grouping of fired bullets found at one of the Union corps hospital sites behind the battlefield. Some of these projectiles were probably stray shots that fell behind the Yankee lines; however, others were undoubtedly removed from wounded soldiers.

4   Bullets embedded in wood from trees.

5   "Wounded" trees in the Culp's Hill area.

    A.   Courtesy of Mr. William A. Frassanito. Brady and Company stereo #2391 taken on or about July 15, 1863.

    B.   Courtesy of Mr. William A. Frassanito. Peter S. and Hanson E. Weaver stereo #71, ca. 1864.

    C.   Tyson Brothers stereo #522, ca. 1865 (NPS).

    D.   Tyson Brothers stereo #523, ca. 1865 (NPS).

    E.   Tyson Brothers stereo #533, ca. 1865 (NPS).

A

B

C

E

D

APPENDIX 1

Organization and armament of the Army of the Potomac at Gettysburg, excluding the artillery.

This listing of the weapons carried by the cavalry and infantry regiments of the Army of the Potomac was compiled from the "Quarterly Summary Statements of Ordnance and Ordnance Stores" in Record Group 156, Records of the Office of the Chief of Ordnance, National Archives and Records Administration. The statements for the 2nd Quarter ending June 30, 1863 were those that were used. (Unfortunately, no similar Confederate records exist.)

The designation ".58" is meant to indicate that the regiment was armed with Springfield rifle muskets, model 1855 or 1861, National Armory or contract, caliber .58, or U.S. rifles, model 1840 or 1845, caliber .58. The weapons shown in parenthesis are listed on the statements in quantities of less than ten and may have been part of the regimental baggage as opposed to having seen use on the firing line.

Army of the Potomac

Major General George G. Meade

I Corps: Major General John F. Reynolds

First Division: Brigadier General James S. Wadsworth
    1st Brigade: Brigadier General Solomon Meredith

19th Indiana	.58
24th Michigan	.58
2nd Wisconsin	Austrian .54
6th Wisconsin	.58
7th Wisconsin	Austrian .58, Austrian .54, (.58)

    2nd Brigade: Brigadier General Lysander Cutler

7th Indiana	Enfield .577
76th New York	.58, Enfield .577
84th New York	.58
95th New York	Enfield .577, Austrian .54
147th New York	Enfield .577
56th Pennsylvania	.58

Second Division: Brigadier General John C. Robinson
    1st Brigade: Brigadier General Gabriel R. Paul

16th Maine	Enfield .577
13th Massachusetts	Enfield .577, (.58)
94th New York	.58, (Enfield .577)
104th New York	Enfield .577, (.58)
107th Pennsylvania	Enfield .577, Austrian .54

    2nd Brigade: Brigadier General Henry Baxter

12th Massachusetts	Enfield .577
83rd New York	.58, Enfield .577
97th New York	Enfield .577
11th Pennsylvania	.69 rifled
88th Pennsylvania	Enfield .577, .69 smoothbore, (.58)
90th Pennsylvania	.58

Third Division: Brigadier General Thomas A. Rowley, Major General Abner Doubleday
    1st Brigade: Colonel Chapman Biddle

80th New York	Austrian .54
121st Pennsylvania	.58
142nd Pennsylvania	.58, Enfield .577

151st Pennsylvania	Enfield .577
2nd Brigade: Colonel Roy Stone	
143rd Pennsylvania	.58, Enfield .577
149th Pennsylvania	Enfield .577
150th Pennsylvania	.58, Enfield .577
3rd Brigade: Brigadier General George J. Stannard	
12th Vermont	.58
13th Vermont	.58
14th Vermont	Austrian .54
15th Vermont	.58
16th Vermont	.58, (Enfield .577)

II Corps: Major General Winfield S. Hancock

First Division: Brigadier General John C. Caldwell

1st Brigade: Colonel Edward E. Cross	
5th New Hampshire	Enfield .577, (.58)
61st New York	Enfield .577
81st Pennsylvania	.58, .69 smoothbore
148th Pennsylvania	.58
2nd Brigade: Colonel Patrick Kelly	
28th Massachusetts	.58, Enfield .577
63rd New York	.69 smoothbore
69th New York	.69 smoothbore
88th New York	.69 smoothbore, (.58)
116th Pennsylvania	.69 smoothbore
3rd Brigade: Brigadier General Samuel K. Zook	
52nd New York	.58, Enfield .577
57th New York	.58, Enfield .577
66th New York	Enfield .577
140th Pennsylvania	.58
4th Brigade: Colonel John R. Brooke	
27th Connecticut	.58, Austrian .54
64th New York	Austrian .54
53rd Pennsylvania	.58
145th Pennsylvania	.69 smoothbore
2nd Delaware	.58

Second Division: Brigadier General John Gibbon

1st Brigade: Brigadier General William Harrow	
19th Maine	.58
1st Minnesota	.58, Sharps Rifles, .69 rifled, .69 smoothbore
15th Massachusetts	.58, .69 rifled
82nd New York	.58, Enfield .577, .69 smoothbore
2nd Brigade: Brigadier General Alexander S. Webb	
69th Pennsylvania	.58, Enfield .577, .69 rifled
71st Pennsylvania	.58
72nd Pennsylvania	.58, Enfield .577, Austrian .58
106th Pennsylvania	.58, French .58, .69 smoothbore
3rd Brigade: Colonel Norman J. Hall	
19th Massachusetts	.58, Enfield .577
20th Massachusetts	Enfield .577, (.58)
42nd New York	.58, Enfield .577
59th New York	.58, Enfield .577
7th Michigan	.58

1st Company Massachusetts SS	Sharps Rifles, Merrill Rifles

Third Division: Brigadier General Alexander Hays
    1st Brigade: Colonel Samuel S. Carroll

14th Indiana	.58, Enfield .577
4th Ohio	.58, Enfield .577, .69 smoothbore, .69 English smoothbore
8th Ohio	.58, Enfield .577, .69 smoothbore
7th West Virginia	.58, Enfield .577

    2nd Brigade: Colonel Thomas A. Smyth

14th Connecticut	.58, Sharps Rifles
10th New York	.58, (U.S. .54, Enfield .577, .69 smoothbore)
108th New York	.58
1st Delaware	.58, Enfield .577, .69 rifled
12th New Jersey	.69 smoothbore

    3rd Brigade: Colonel George L. Willard

39th New York	Enfield .577, French .577
111th New York	.58
125th New York	.58
126th New York	.58

III Corps: Major General Daniel E. Sickles

First Division: Major General David B. Birney
    1st Brigade: Brigadier General Charles K. Graham

57th Pennsylvania	Austrian .54, (Enfield .577)
63rd Pennsylvania	Austrian .54, Austrian .577
68th Pennsylvania	Enfield .577
105th Pennsylvania	.58
114th Pennsylvania	.58, Enfield .577
141st Pennsylvania	.58, Austrian .54

    2nd Brigade: Brigadier General J. H. Hobart Ward

20th Indiana	.58, Enfield .577
3rd Maine	.58
4th Maine	Austrian .54
86th New York	Enfield .577
124th New York	Enfield .577
99th Pennsylvania	Austrian .54
1st United States SS	Sharps Rifles
2nd United States SS	Sharps Rifles

    3rd Brigade: Colonel P. Regis DeTrobriand

17th Maine	Enfield .577
3rd Michigan	Austrian .54, .58, (Enfield .577)
5th Michigan	Austrian .54
40th New York	Enfield .577
110th Pennsylvania	.58, Enfield .577

Second Division: Brigadier General A. A. Humphreys
    1st Brigade: Brigadier General Joseph B. Carr

1st Massachusetts	.58
11th Massachusetts	.69 smoothbore
16th Massachusetts	Enfield .577, .58
11th New Jersey	Enfield .577, Austrian .58, Austrian .577, .69 smoothbore
12th New Hampshire	.58, .69 smoothbore
26th Pennsylvania	Austrian .54
84th Pennsylvania	.58, Enfield .577

2nd Brigade: Colonel William R. Brewster
70th New York	.58
71st New York	.58
72nd New York	.58
73rd New York	.58
74th New York	Enfield .577
120th New York	.58

3rd Brigade: Colonel George C. Burling
2nd New Hampshire	.58, Sharps Rifle
5th New Jersey	Austrian .58, Austrian .54
6th New Jersey	.58, (Enfield .577, Austrian .58)
7th New Jersey	.58, Enfield .577, .69 smoothbore, (Austrian .54)
8th New Jersey	.58 (Enfield .577, Austrian .58)
115th Pennsylvania	Enfield .577

V Corps: Major General George Sykes

First Division: Brigadier General James Barnes
1st Brigade: Colonel William Tilton
18th Massachusetts	.58
22nd Massachusetts	.58
1st Michigan	.58, (Enfield .577)
118th Pennsylvania	.58

2nd Brigade: Colonel Jacob B. Sweitzer
9th Massachusetts	.69 rifled, .69 smoothbore
32nd Massachusetts	Enfield .577, (.58)
4th Michigan	.58, (Enfield .577)
62nd Pennsylvania	.58

3rd Brigade: Colonel Strong Vincent
20th Maine	.58, Enfield .577
16th Michigan	.58, Enfield .577
44th New York	.58, (Enfield .577)
83rd Pennsylvania	.58

Second Division: Brigadier General Romeyn B. Ayres
1st Brigade: Colonel Hannibal Day
3rd United States	.58
4th United States	.58
6th United States	.58
12th United States	.58
14th United States	.58

2nd Brigade: Colonel Sidney Burbank
2nd United States	.58
7th United States	.58
10th United States	.58
11th United States	.58, Enfield .577
17th United States	.58

3rd Brigade: Brigadier General Stephen H. Weed
140th New York	.58, Enfield .577
146th New York	.58
91st Pennsylvania	.58
155th Pennsylvania	.69 smoothbore

Third Division: Brigadier General Samuel W. Crawford
1st Brigade: Colonel William McCandless

1st Pennslvania Reserves (30th Regt.)	.69 rifled
2nd Pennsylvania Reserves (31st Regt.)	Enfield .577, .69 rifled
6th Pennsylvania Reserves (35th Regt.)	.58
13th Pennsylvania Reserves (42nd Regt. Bucktails)	Enfield .577, .69 smoothbore, Sharps Rifles, (.58)

3rd Brigade: Colonel Joseph W. Fisher

5th Pennsylvania Reserves (34th Regt.)	.69 smoothbore
9th Pennsylvania Reserves (38th Regt.)	.69 smoothbore
10th Pennsylvania Reserves (39th Regt.)	Enfield .577
11th Pennsylvania Reserves (40th Regt.)	.69 rifled
12th Pennsylvania Reserves (41st Regt.)	.69 rifled

VI Corps: Major General John Sedgwick

First Division: Brigadier General Horatio G. Wright

1st Brigade: Brigadier General A. T. A. Torbert

1st New Jersey	.58
2nd New Jersey	.58
3rd New Jersey	.58, .69 smoothbore
15th New Jersey	Enfield .577

2nd Brigade: Brigadier General Joseph J. Bartlett

5th Maine	.58, (Enfield .577)
95th Pennsylvania	.58
96th Pennsylvania	.58, Enfield .577
121st New York	Enfield .577

3rd Brigade: Brigadier General David A. Russell

6th Maine	.58
49th Pennsylvania	Austrian .54
119th Pennsylvania	.58
5th Wisconsin	Austrian .54

Second Division: Brigadier General Albion P. Howe

2nd Brigade: Colonel Lewis A. Grant

2nd Vermont	.58
3rd Vermont	.58
4th Vermont	Enfield .577
5th Vermont	.58
6th Vermont	Enfield .577

3rd Brigade: Brigadier General Thomas H. Neill

7th Maine	.58
43rd New York	Enfield .577, Austrian .54
49th New York	.58, Enfield .577
77th New York	Enfield .577
61st Pennsylvania	.58

Third Division: Major General John Newton

1st Brigade: Brigadier General Alexander Shaler

65th New York	.58
67th New York	.58
122nd New York	.58, Enfield .577
23rd Pennsylvania	Austrian .54
82nd Pennsylvania	Enfield .577

2nd Brigade: Colonel Henry L. Eustis

7th Massachusetts	Enfield .577
10th Massachusetts	.58, Enfield .577
37th Massachusetts	.58
2nd Rhode Island	.58

3rd Brigade: Brigadier General Frank Wheaton

62nd New York	Austrian .54, (Enfield .577)
93rd Pennsylvania	.69 rifled, .69 smoothbore
98th Pennsylvania	.58, French .58
102nd Pennsylvania	.58, .69 smoothbore
139th Pennsylvania	.69 rifled

XI Corps: Major General Oliver O. Howard

First Division: Brigadier General Francis C. Barlow

1st Brigade: Colonel Leopold Von Gilsa

41st New York	Enfield .577
54th New York	Enfield .577
68th New York	.58
153rd Pennsylvania	Austrian .58

2nd Brigade: Brigadier General Adelbert Ames

17th Connecticut	Enfield .577
25th Ohio	Enfield .577
75th Ohio	Enfield .577, (.58)
107th Ohio	Enfield .577, .58

Second Division: Brigadier General Adolph Von Steinwehr

1st Brigade: Colonel Charles R. Coster

134th New York	.58, Enfield .577, .69 rifled foreign
154th New York	Enfield .577
27th Pennsylvania	Enfield .577, .69 smoothbore
73rd Pennsylvania	.58, Enfield .577, Austrian .58, Austrian .54

2nd Brigade: Colonel Orland Smith

33rd Massachusetts	Enfield .577
136th New York	Enfield .577
55th Ohio	Enfield .577
73rd Ohio	Enfield .577

Third Division: Major General Carl Schurz

1st Brigade: Brigadier General Alexander Schimmelfennig

82nd Illinois	Enfield .577
45th New York	U.S. .54
157th New York	Enfield .577
61st Ohio	Enfield .577, .58, .69 rifled
74th Pennsylvania	.58, Enfield .577, French .58

2nd Brigade: Colonel W. Krzyzanowski

58th New York	Enfield .577
119th New York	Enfield .577
82nd Ohio	Enfield .577, .58
75th Pennsylvania	.58

26th Wisconsin	Enfield .577

XII Corps: Major General Henry W. Slocum

First Division: Brigadier General Alpheus S. Williams
    1st Brigade: Colonel Archibald L. McDougall

5th Connecticut	.58, (Enfield .577)
20th Connecticut	.58
3rd Maryland	.58, Enfield .577
123rd New York	.58, Enfield .577
145th New York	.58
46th Pennsylvania	.58

    2nd Brigade: Brigadier General Henry H. Lockwood

1st Maryland, Potomac Home Brigade	Enfield .577
1st Maryland, Eastern Shore	Enfield .577
150th New York	.58, Austrian .54

    3rd Brigade: Brigadier General Thomas H. Ruger

27th Indiana	.58, Austrian .58
2nd Massachusetts	Enfield .577
13th New Jersey	.58, Enfield .577
107th New York	.58
3rd Wisconsin	.58, (Enfield .577)

Second Division: Brigadier General John W. Geary
    1st Brigade: Colonel Charles Candy

5th Ohio	.58
7th Ohio	.58
29th Ohio	Enfield .577
66th Ohio	.58
28th Pennsylvania	.58, Enfield .577
147th Pennsylvania	.58, Enfield .577

    2nd Brigade: Colonel George A. Cobham

29th Pennsylvania	.58, (Enfield .577)
109th Pennsylvania	.58, (Enfield .577)
111th Pennsylvania	Enfield .577

    3rd Brigade: Brigadier General George S. Greene

60th New York	Enfield .577
78th New York	Enfield .577, (.58)
102nd New York	.58
137th New York	Enfield .577
149th New York	Enfield .577, (.58)

Cavalry Corps: Major General Alfred Pleasonton

First Division: Brigadier General John Buford
    1st Brigade: Colonel William Gamble

8th Illinois	Sharps*, Colt .36, Colt .44
12th Illinois	Burnside, Colt .44
3rd Indiana	Gallager, Sharps, Colt .44
8th New York	Sharps, Colt .44

    2nd Brigade: Colonel Thomas C. Devin

6th New York	Sharps, Colt .44
9th New York	Sharps, (Smith), Colt .44
17th Pennsylvania	Merrill, Smith, Colt .44, Colt .36, Remington .36
3rd West Virginia	Gallager, Smith, Colt .44, Remington .36

Reserve Brigade: Brigadier General Wesley Merritt
6th Pennsylvania	Sharps, Colt .44, Colt .36
1st United States	Sharps, Colt .44
2nd United States	Sharps, Colt .44
5th United States	Sharps, Colt .44
6th United States	Sharps, Colt .44, Colt .36

Second Division: Brigadier General David McM. Gregg
1st Brigade: Colonel John B. McIntosh
1st Maryland	Burnside, Sharps, Colt .44
1st Massachusetts	Sharps, Colt .44, Remington .44
1st New Jersey	Burnside, Smith, Colt .44
1st Pennsylvania	Sharps, Burnside, Colt .44, Colt .36
3rd Pennsylvania	Sharps, Colt .44, Remington .44, Colt .36

2nd Brigade: Colonel Pennock Huey
2nd New York	Sharps, Colt .44
4th New York	Sharps, Burnside, Colt .44, Remington .44
6th Ohio	Burnside, (Sharps, Smith), Colt .44, Remington .44
8th Pennsylvania	Sharps, Colt .44, Remington .36, Allen's .44

3rd Brigade: Colonel J. Irvin Gregg
1st Maine	Burnside, Sharps, Colt .44
10th New York	Sharps, Colt .44, Colt .36
4th Pennsylvania	Sharps, Colt .44, Colt .36
16th Pennsylvania	Sharps, Colt .44, Remington .44

Third Division: Brigadier General Judson Kilpatrick
1st Brigade: Brigadier General Elon J. Farnsworth
5th New York	Sharps, Colt .44
18th Pennsylvania	Burnside, Colt .44
1st Vermont	Sharps, Colt .44, Remington .44
1st West Virginia	Sharps, (Burnside), Colt .44

2nd Brigade: Brigadier General George A. Custer
1st Michigan	Sharps, (Burnside), Colt .44
5th Michigan	Spencer Rifles, Colt .44
6th Michigan	Spencer Rifles, Burnside, Colt .44
7th Michigan	Burnside, Colt .44

Headquarters Guard
1st Ohio	Sharps, Colt .44, Colt .36, Remington .36, Whitney .36

Provost Guard, Army HQ
2nd Pennsylvania	Sharps, Colt .44

* All Sharps weapons listed for the Cavalry Corps are carbines.

Ordnance Supplies.

Head-Quarters, Army of the Potomac,

Camp near Falmouth, Va., March 25, 1863

General Orders, }
No. 20.   }

On and after the receipt of this order, all requisitions for ordnance stores will be made in duplicate.

Those for infantry and cavalry, after being signed by the colonels of the regiments, will be presented to the acting ordnance officers of divisions, who will make consolidated requisitions for all stores required for their divisions. These consolidated requisitions, after being signed by the General commanding the division, and, when for the cavalry, by the General commanding the corps, also will be presented to the chief ordnance officer at these Head-quarters, and after being approved by him will be issued upon. In all cases the division ordnance officers will present, along with the consolidated requisitions, the original regimental requisitions, or copies of the same, for the examination of the division commanders, and to the chief ordnance officer, at these Head-quarters, for his approval, to be forwarded to Washington.

All requisitions for ordnance and ordnance stores for batteries, after being signed by the captain of the battery, the chief of artillery of the corps and the chief of artillery of this army, will be presented to the chief ordnance officer at these Head-quarters, and after being approved by him will be issued upon. Blanks for requisitions can be obtained from division ordnance officers, and officers requiring stores are directed to fill up all the columns according to the printed headings, and to follow all the printed directions therein. Requisitions, when the printed form has been mutilated and changed, will not be approved.

Division ordnance officers will be held responsible that the following supply of ammunition is kept constantly on hand. For infantry, 140 rounds, with that in the cartridge boxes. For cavalry, 100 rounds of carbine, and 40 rounds pistol, with that in the cartridge boxes. For artillery, 250 rounds, with that in the ammunition chest. The 20 rounds infantry ammunition heretofore carried in the knapsacks of the men, after that is expended which they now have in their knapsacks, will not thereafter be carried by the men; but immediately before an action, Generals commanding divisions will see that 20 extra rounds are issued to the men, to be carried in their pockets.

The wagons containing the reserve ammunition will be under the control of the division ordnance officers. Ammunition wagons will be distinguished by a horizontal stripe, six inches wide, painted on each side of the cover; for artillery ammunition, red; for cavalry, yellow; for infantry, light blue. The wagons will also be distinctly marked with the number of the corps and division to which they belong, and the kind and calibre of ammunition contained. The main depot for the army will be designated by a crimson flag marked "Ordnance Depot, U. S. A." Upon the march, or when the brigades are widely separated from each other, the wagons containing the reserve ammunition for each brigade may, at the discretion of the division commander, be turned over to the brigade quarter-master, who will draw his supplies from the division ordnance officer.

In time of action, division ordnance officers will be careful to get explicit instructions from their division commanders in regard to the disposition to be made of their trains, and they will themselves remain with their trains to attend to the issue of ammunition. If it should be necessary, during a prolonged action, to replenish the trains, the division ordnance officers will be informed where the ammunition can be obtained, and they will send for it a portion of their trains, in charge of a competent officer or non-commissioned officer, with a correct list of the *kind*, and *amount of each kind* they require.

Division ordnance officers will keep themselves constantly informed of the condition of the regiments in their division; and when deficiencies in ordnance stores are found to exist, they will see that requisitions are promptly made to supply them. They will, on the 15th of each month, submit, for the examination of the General commanding their division, to be forwarded through corps Head-quarters to the chief ordnance officer at these Head-quarters, a report of the number, kind, and calibre of arms in each regiment of their division, and of the amount, kind, and calibre of ammunition in their trains.

Unserviceable and condemned ordnance stores, which are to be turned in, will not pass through division ordnance officers. When the companies of a regiment have such stores to turn in, they will first turn them over to the quarter-master of the regiment, who will, as will also be done in all other cases, turn them in at the ordnance depot, or send them to an arsenal, transmitting with them invoices and receipts, stating the exact condition of the stores, as shown by the inspector's report.

So much of General Orders No. 152, of August 9th, 1862, from Head-quarters, Army of the Potomac, as conflicts with this order, is hereby revoked.

The officer detailed as division ordnance officer will be relieved from all other duty, and will report at the Head-quarters of his division. He will select from the privates and non-commissioned officers of his division, a competent clerk and an acting ordnance sergeant, who will be detailed for extra-duty by the division commander, to report to the ordnance officer.

When the provisions of General Orders No. 189, of November 18th, 1862, from the War Department, are not sufficient to keep in repair the arms of a brigade, the brigade commander will detail an armorer from his brigade, to report to the division ordnance officer, who will supply him with a set of armorer's tools.

The extra-duty men thus detailed, will be under the charge of the division ordnance officer, and will be borne on his extra-duty rolls.

BY COMMAND OF MAJOR GENERAL HOOKER:

S. WILLIAMS,
Assistant Adjutant General.

OFFICIAL:

Captain, A. D. C.

Source: Records of the Adjutant General's Office, AGO Collection of Orders (NARA).

APPENDIX 3

Powder charges for standard Civil War small arms cartridges.

Union

.69 cal. rifled musket, expanding ball	– 70	grains
.58 cal. rifle musket, expanding ball	– 60	"
.69 cal. smoothbore musket, round ball	– 110	"
.44 cal. Army revolver, elongated ball	– 30	"
.36 cal. Navy revolver, elongated ball	– 17	"
.52 cal. Sharps carbine, elongated ball	– 50	"

Source: *The Ordnance Manual for the Use of the Officers of the United States Army* (Third Edition, Philadelphia, 1861) 270. The *Ordnance Manual* does not list the .577 cal. Enfield rifle musket or the .54 cal. rifle musket. The powder charges for these were both 60 grains.

Confederate

.54 cal. Mississippi rifle	– 70	grains
.577 cal. Enfield rifle musket	– 70	"
.58 cal. rifle musket	– 75	"
.69 cal. rifled musket	– 80	"
.69 cal. smoothbore musket, round ball	– 100	"
.69 cal. smoothbore musket, buck and ball	– 110	"
.54 cal. Merrill carbine	– 50	"
.52 cal. Sharps carbine	– 60	"
.50 cal. Maynard carbine	– 55	"
.44 cal. Colt army pistol	– 30	"
.36 cal. Colt navy pistol	– 17	"
.54 cal. Horseman's pistol	– 30	"

Source: *The Field Manual for the Use of the Officers on Ordnance Duty* (Richmond, 1862).

NOTES

1. Rimfire and some other types of cartridges also included the primer. See Part III, Sections H and I.

2. This deterioration is normally speeded up by the bullet having been buried in the ground. However, depending upon the exact chemical make-up and moisture content of the soil, and other objects or materials that may have been buried with the bullet, the rate at which lead oxide forms varies greatly. A patina does not indicate whether the bullet is "real" or a reproduction.

3. The following books provide additional information on early projectile experiments and the different systems of small arms:

    Major Alfred Mordecai, *Military Commission to Europe in 1855 and 1856* (Washington, 1861); *Reports of Experiments with Small Arms for the Military Service by Officers of the Ordnance Department, U.S. Army* (Washington, 1856); J. Schön, *Rifled Infantry Arms. A Brief Description of the Modern System of Small Arms as adopted in the Various European Armies* (Dresden, 1855); and Cadmus M. Wilcox, *Rifles and Rifle Practice* (New York, 1861).

4. *The Ordnance Manual for the Use of the Officers of the United States Army* (Third Edition, Philadelphia, 1861), 266.

5. Col. H.K. Craig to Lt. T.J. Rodman, May 30, 1854, "Letters Received at Allegheny Arsenal" (National Archives and Records Admin., Record Group 156 Records of the Office of the Chief of Ordnance, hereafter cited as NARA, RG 156).

6. Col. H.K. Craig to Lt. T.J. Rodman, Jan. 23, 1855, "Letters Received at Allegheny Arsenal"; Col. H.K. Craig to Maj. John Symington, Jan. 16, 1859, "Letters Received at Allegheny Arsenal"; Maj. Alfred Mordecai to Col. H.K. Craig, March 23, 1859, "Letters Sent from Watervliet Arsenal"; Col. H.K. Craig to Capt. Josiah Gorgas, Sept. 1, 1860, "Letters Received from the Ordnance Office at Frankford Arsenal," and Gen. James W. Ripley to Col. D.D. Tompkins, June 4, 1861, "Miscellaneous Letters Sent by the Chief of Ordnance" (NARA, RG 156).

7. *Ordnance Manual*, 266.

8. Arthur B. Hawes, *Rifle Ammunition*, (London, 1859), 11-19.

9. Bvt. Maj. T.T.S. Laidley to J.D. Custer, June 25, 1862, "Letters Sent from Frankford Arsenal" (NARA, RG 156).

10. "Statements of Purchases of Ordnance, Class VIII, 1862-1865" (NARA, RG 156).

11. William LeRoy Broun, "Confederate Ordnance During the War," *Southern Historical Society Papers*, XXVI, 366-67.

12. Abstract from returns of the Army of the Potomac, June 10 – July 31, 1863, U.S. War Department, *Official Records of the War of the Rebellion*, XXVII, Part 1, 151. All citations from the *Official Records* are from Vol. XXVII. Hereafter they will be cited as "*OR*, Part __, p.__." The breakdown by corps is listed below:

I	Corps –	8,716
II	Corps –	11,436
III	Corps –	10,451
V	Corps –	11,157
VI	Corps –	13,530
XI	Corps –	8,648
XII	Corps –	7,672

    Total   71,922   infantrymen "present for duty equipped" June 30, 1863.

13. See Appendix 2.

14. Report of Col. Hiram Berdan, July 29, 1863, *OR*, Part 1, 516; Report of Brig. Gen. John W. Geary, July 29, 1863, *OR*, Part 1, 833; and Report of Lt. Joseph G. Rosengarten, July 19, 1863, *OR*, Part 1, 265.

15. *OR*, Part 3, 416-17.

16. Although dated over a year after the battle of Gettysburg, the letter below gives some insight into the "care" afforded extra ammunition by some soldiers of the Army of the Potomac:

Ordnance Office Watervliet Arsenal
West Troy, Aug. 11th, 1864

Genl. G.D. Ramsay
Chief of Ordnance
Washington

General:

In conversation with Capt. Cooley of the 11th Infty. recently, he volunteered the remark that there was great wastage of ammunition in the Army of the Potomac, where he had been serving, in consequence of the orders frequently given to receive 50 rounds per man, when the men could only take care of 40 rounds in their boxes. He said that the men would throw away the extra bundle as soon as they got a chance. I think it is worth while to mention this, as you may deem it proper to make inquiry upon the subject in view of the large issues just now.

Very Respectfully,
Your Obt. Servt.
P.V. Hagner
Lt. Col. of Ordn.
Comdg.

"Letters Sent from Watervliet Arsenal" (NARA, RG 156).

17. See General Orders No. 30, Head-Quarters, Army of the Potomac, dated March 25, 1863, appended hereto. This order was still in effect during the Gettysburg campaign. Additionally, see Edward Steere, *The Wilderness Campaign* (New York, 1960), 25. Meade's plans in 1864 called for fifty rounds on the person and 100 rounds per man in the wagons.

18. *OR*, Part 3, 542.

19. Report of Brig. Gen. John W. Geary, July 29, 1863, *OR*, Part 1, 833.

20. Report of Lt. Joseph G. Rosengarten, July 19, 1863, *OR*, Part 1, 265.

21. This is the initial strength at the opening of the battle. Deducting casualties would actually increase the number of rounds per man expended.

22. Report of Brig. Gen. John C. Robinson, July 18, 1863, *OR*, Part 1, 290.

23. Report of Col. Joshua L. Chamberlain, July 6, 1863, *OR*, Part 1, 624.

24. Report of Col. Hiram Berdan, July 29, 1863, *OR*, Part 1, 516.

25. References to this fact in Ordnance Department records are numerous. The following from "Letters Sent from Watervliet Arsenal" is an example:

Watervliet Arsenal
May 27th 1862

Captain M.R. Stevenson
Comdg. Co. "B," 7th U.S. Infantry
Madison Barracks, N.Y.

Sir:

I have the honor to inform you that Sanders Lansing M.S.K. and Paymaster at this Arsenal, has handed me your letter of the 21st inst. returning ammunition issued to your address from this post because of the size of the balls being 57/100 inch Calibre.

Respecting this matter I have to inform you that no cartridges are made of .58 Calibre they are all of .57 Calibre, which makes them answerable for the Enfield muskets of .57 and the American muskets of .58 Calibre. The advantage of this is that one kind of ammunition answers for two kinds of arms and gives greater ease and rapidity in loading the American musket. For the same reasons we have but one kind of ammunition for the American rifle of .54 and the Austrian rifle of .55 Calibre as we only furnish rifle cartridges of .54 Calibre.

For the reasons explained I have directed the M.S.K. to remark the <u>3 boxes</u> containing 3000 rifle musket cartridges <u>.57 Cal.</u> and return to your address pursuant to order for supplies from Washington.

Respectfully I am Sir
Your Obt. Servt.
W.A. Thornton
Major of Ord.

26. Report of E.S. Allin, Nov. 21, 1861, "Correspondence and Reports Relating to Experiments, Class VIII" (NARA, RG 156).

27. "Statements of Purchases of Ordnance, Class VIII, 1862" (NARA, RG 156).

28. Col. Berkeley R. Lewis, *Small Arms and Ammunition in the United States Service, 1776-1865* (Washington, 1956), 200.

29. Lt. Col. Wm. Maynadier to Maj. R.H.K. Whiteley, April 8, 1863, "Letters Received at Allegheny Arsenal" (NARA, RG 156).

30. Letters Patent No. 37,145, Dec. 9, 1862 (U.S. Patent Office).

31. Lt. Col. P.V. Hagner to Gen. G.D. Ramsay, Aug. 27, 1864, "Experiments with Powder, Ammunition, etc., Class VIII" (NARA, RG 156).

32. Samuel Toombs, *New Jersey Troops in the Gettysburg Campaign* (Orange, N.J., 1888), 294.

33. "Ledgers of Receipts on Orders and Contracts, Class VIII, 1862" (NARA, RG 156). See Part III, Section I, specimen #4.

34. Capt. S.V. Benet to Gen. James W. Ripley, May 23, 1862, "Experiments with Inventions, Class VIII" (NARA, RG 156).

35. Capt. L. Schirmer to Edwin M. Stanton, Nov. 4, 1862, *ibid.*

36. Martin A. Haynes, *History of the Second Regiment, New Hampshire Volunteer Infantry, in the War of the Rebellion* (Lakeport, N.H., 1896), 159.

37. Reuben Shaler to Gen. James W. Ripley, Aug. 15, 1861, "Experiments with Inventions, Class VIII" (NARA, RG 156).

38. "Statements of Purchases of Ordnance, Class VIII, 1862" (NARA, RG 156).

39. *Ibid.*

40. Report of Lt. Joseph G. Rosengarten, July 19, 1863, *OR*, Part 1, 265.

41. Edwin B. Coddington, *The Gettysburg Campaign, A Study in Command* (New York, 1968), 249.

42. *Ibid.*, 258-59.

43. Samual Jackson to Gen. G.D. Ramsay, Feb. 1, 1864, "Experiments with Powder, Ammunition, etc., Class VIII" (NARA, RG 156). Jackson later patented his own type of Gallager cartridge.

44. Letters Patent No. 34,061, Jan. 7, 1862 (U.S. Patent Office).

45. Horace Edwin Hayden, "Explosive or Poisoned Musket or Rifle Balls," *Southern Historical Society Papers*, VIII, 24.

46. Coddington, *The Gettysburg Campaign*, 248-49; Edward J. Stackpole, *They Met at Gettysburg* (Harrisburg, Pa., 1956), 115.

47. Coddington, *The Gettysburg Campaign*, 252.

48. William LeRoy Broun, "Southern Genius," *Southern Historical Society Papers*, XVI, 289.

49. J. Holt to Edwin M. Stanton, Sept. 17, 1863, *OR*, Part 2, 193.

50. Gen. Robert E. Lee to Jefferson Davis, June 18, 1863, *OR*, Part 2, 295.

51. Gen. Alfred Pleasonton to Gen. S. Williams, June 20, 1863, *OR*, Part 1, 911. Pleasonton, commanding the Union Cavalry Corps, reported that a "rebel infantry soldier [captured at Aldie, Va.] had 200 cartridges in his haversack," but there is no way to know if this was typical of Lee's soldiers.

52. Gen. Robert E. Lee to Jefferson Davis, June 18, 1863, *OR*, Part 2, 300.

53. Report of Gen. Robert E. Lee, Jan. 20, 1864, *ibid.*, 325.

54. Gen. Winfield S. Hancock to Gen. George G. Meade, July 3, 1863, *OR*, Part 1, 366. It is interesting to note the comment by Hancock in regard to his wounding: "The enemy must be short of ammunition, as I was shot with a tenpenny nail." The truth of the matter was that a bullet hit his saddle and drove a nail from his saddle into his leg.

55. Josiah Gorgas, *The Ordnance Manual for the Use of Officers of the Confederate States Army* (Charleston, 1863), 253.

56. 1st Lt. Peters S. Michie to Brig. Gen. Richard Delafield, Chief Engineer USA, October 1865 (U.S. Military Academy Library, West Point, NY).

57. Report of Lt. Col. L.H. Scruggs, Aug. 8, 1863, *OR*, Part 2, 391.

58. Report of Lt. Col. P.A. Work, July 9, 1863, *ibid.*, 410.

59. Report of Gen. George H. Steuart, Sept. 2, 1863, *ibid.*, 510; Report of Gen. J.A. Walker, Aug. 17, 1863, *ibid.*, 519; Report of Col. J.H.S. Funk, Aug. 18, 1863, *ibid.*, 526; Report of Lt. Col. Daniel M. Shriver, July 19, 1863, *ibid.*, 528; Report of Capt. J.B. Golladay, July 16, 1863, *ibid.*, 530; Report of Lt. Col. L.H.N. Salyer, July 6, 1863, *ibid.*, 539.

60. Report of Capt. J.B. Golladay, July 16, 1863, *ibid.*, 530.

61. Report of Maj. Eugene Blackford, July 17, 1863, *ibid.*, 598.

62. *Ibid.*

63. Report of Gen. Henry Heth, Sept. 13, 1863, *ibid.*, 639.

64. Report of Maj. J. Jones, Aug. 9, 1863, *ibid.*, 643.

65. Stackpole, *They Met at Gettysburg*, 279.

66. Report of Gen. J.E.B. Stuart, Aug. 20, 1863, *OR*, Part 2, 696-98.

67. *Ibid.*

68. Glenn Tucker, *High Tide at Gettysburg* (1958), 324.

BIBLIOGRAPHY

Bates, Samuel P. *History of the Pennsylvania Volunteers, 1861-1865.* 5 vols., Harrisburg, Pa., 1869-71.

Broun, William LeRoy. "Confederate Ordnance During the War," *Southern Historical Society Papers*, XXVI, 365-376.

____. "Southern Genius," *Southern Historical Society Papers*, XVI, 286-89.

Coddington, Edwin B. *The Gettysburg Campaign, A Study in Command.* New York, 1968.

____. *The Field Manual for the Use of Officers on Ordnance Duty.* Richmond, 1862.

Frassanito, William A. Gettysburg: A Journey in Time. New York, 1975.

Gorgas, Josiah. *The Ordnance Manual for the Use of Officers of the Confederate States Army.* Charleston, 1863.

Hawes, Arthur B. *Rifle Ammunition.* London, 1859.

Hayden, Horace Edwin. "Explosive or Poisoned Musket or Rifle Balls," *Southern Historical Society Papers*, VIII, 18-28.

Haynes, Martin A. *History of the Second Regiment, New Hampshire Volunteer Infantry, in the War of the Rebellion.* Lakeport, N.H., 1896.

____. *Instructions for making Quarterly Returns of Ordnance and Ordnance Stores.* Washington, 1863.

Lewis, Berkeley R. *Small Arms and Ammunition in the United States Service, 1776-1865.* Washington, 1956.

____. *Metallic Ammunition for the Springfield Breech-Loading Rifle-Musket. Ordnance Memoranda No. 8.* Washington, 1870.

Mordecai, Alfred. *Military Commission to Europe in 1855 and 1856.* Washington, 1861.

____. *The Ordnance Manual for the Use of the Officers of the United States Army.* Philadelphia, 1861.

____. Records of the Adjutant General's Office, No. 94; Records of the Office of the Chief of Ordnance, No. 156, National Archives and Records Administration.

____. *Reports of Experiments with Small Arms for the Military Service by Officers of the Ordnance Department, U.S. Army.* Washington, 1856.

Schön, J. *Rifled Infantry Arms. A Brief Description of the Modern System of Small Arms, as adopted in the Various European Armies.* Dresden, 1855.

Stackpole, Edward J. *They Met at Gettysburg.* Harrisburg, Pa., 1956.

Steere, Edward. *The Wilderness Campaign.* New York, 1960.

Toombs, Samuel. *New Jersey Troops in the Gettysburg Campaign.* Orange, N.J., 1888.

Tucker, Glenn. *High Tide at Gettysburg.* 1958.

____. U.S. Department of Commerce, Records of the U.S. Patent Office.

____. U.S. Department of War, *The War of the Rebellion: A Compilation of the Official Records of the Union and Confederate Armies.* 128 vols. and index. Washington, 1880-1901.

Wilcox, Cadmus M. *Rifles and Rifle Practice.* New York, 1861.

THOMAS PUBLICATIONS publishes books about the American Colonial era, the Revolutionary War, the Civil War, and other important topics. For a complete list of titles, please write to:

THOMAS PUBLICATIONS
P.O. Box 3031
Gettysburg, PA 17325

Or visit our website: www.thomaspublications.com